Embrace
ENNOBLING
EXPERIENCES

Thoughts on The Verities Of Life - A Personal Journey

Embrace
ENNOBLING
EXPERIENCES

Thoughts on The Verities Of Life - A Personal Journey

MICHAEL STEVEN PURLES

ARPress
ILLUMINATING IDEAS
EMPOWERING VOICES

ARPress
45 Dan Road Suite 15
Canton MA 02021
  Hotline: 1(888) 821-0229
  Fax: 1(508) 545-7580

Ordering Information:
Quantity sales. Special discounts are available on quantity purchases by corporations, associations, and others. For details, contact the publisher at the address above.

Printed in the United States of America.

ISBN-13:	Softcover	979-8-89676-623-0
	eBook	979-8-89676-624-7

Library of Congress Control Number: 2025924882

Contents

DEDICATION

To Jerry, who will always be my bride, Tracy, Chris, David and Joel, who have been at work since their birth raising me to become a better man.

Author's Note

You might find this exercise a revealing and stimulating one as I did. I have enough gray hair to be able to look ahead and wonder what I will have left my family and others as a legacy. After a lifetime of living is there anything I have that will have value, especially long-term value in the eyes of God? A careful examination of my life and introspection into the corners of my soul reveal that I do have valuable gifts, treasures far beyond earthly value. It became obvious to me that if they are not shared they will have only accomplished a small measure of their being and potential.

What you will find in this work, the experiences, education, and life's "baby steps "of conversion come out of this treasure chest of gifts. The things I will share in this work are very personal. My preference would be to sit together, just the two of us to discuss the sacred things of our hearts. I'd love to get your reaction to my thoughts and to bear personal witness to the truths and tender mercies given me by and of our Father and His Beloved Son. Consider this work the beginning of our discussion, sharing sacred personal experiences together.

This background will be helpful for you as you read. Joseph Smith is the prophet called by the Lord to retore His church in 1830, The Church of Jesus Christ of Latter-Day Saints. Christ's original Church established when He was upon the earth was withdrawn following the persecution and death of all the apostles called to administer His gospel. You will see that I have quoted scriptures from the Bible. In addition, I have quoted from the Book of Mormon, the Doctrine and Covenants (D&C), and the Pearl of Great Price, all latter-day revealed scriptures through Jospeh Smith and other prophets.

Introduction

Ennoble: verb; to make noble, elevate, to raise to the rank of nobility (noble in character, quality, or rank).

I have never questioned that I am God's son. That instruction, initially given when I was a young child, has always been with me. It has warmed my soul from my childhood days like a favorite blanket or being wrapped in a down comforter on a chilly night. Being true to that parentage and birthright has certainly been challenging and sometimes difficult to fully embrace.

I know sin and wished that I didn't, except that I also know forgiveness and thank the Lord with all my heart for that tender mercy and all that I have learned. But, that doesn't mean I am immune to further poor decisions needing repentance. I see others living the life I would like to have, apparently breezing through mortality with all the accomplishment, comfort, and opportunity I think I would love, even for just a day. I know that envy isn't productive, but there are moments . . .

At times, when life conditions are difficult, it is easy to wonder "does He, meaning Heavenly Father, really care about me?" Perhaps He is angry with me, or I am no longer of any value to Him, because of the things I have done. Why won't He help me and yet He helps others? When I'm really feeling sorry for myself, I am tempted to wonder why do others get the blessed, easy, fun, and rewarding pathway? Why am I stuck with the one I have, often ugly, painful, and with misery that doesn't seem to end? Is this right or fair for someone who is a child of God, who is at least trying to be good? In all honesty, I can now answer, "Yes! It is." With that answer, I recognize that my perceptions are not always correct.

In quiet moments, when strong emotions have disappeared and I am able to objectively examine my life, who I am, trying to comprehend my relationship with God, I have heard and felt whisperings of the Spirit that say, "You are His child. He loves you. Your life has value and there is purpose, Godly purpose in the path you are on. It is all according to His will." The key seems to be, "Do I trust Him to get me where I need to be in life?" What if it isn't what I want?

The title of this discussion is *Embrace Ennobling Experiences*. Look at the definition of "ennoble" above. Is this what God, our Father, is trying to accomplish with each of us? We come into this world, each beginning at a similar place, but diverging pathways become apparent early on. Challenges, conditions, and abilities influence the decisions we make. Will we use our agency, no matter what our mortal position is, to search out eternal truths or will we be satisfied to leave things as they are, seeking only to find comfort in our circumstances?

Are our paths different, because we are diverse in our needs and abilities, requiring different experiences to make us "complete" and elevate us to be worthy to return to Him in His home? I submit that our paths are different due to perfect Godly purpose. I believe we came into this world, having had a "lifetime" already of experience, with talents and needs as a part of who we are from our pre-mortal life.

This educational realm begins at birth and ends at, well, when we have graduated and moved on to another university. The number of credit hours varies from one person to another, but each credit hour seems to be important, all a part of a progressive plan. There are two questions that seem so very important about this required course of study:

➤ Why do we have to take it?
➤ What will we get out of it?

I am confident that we knew the answers to these questions before coming here, but due to "pre-mortal amnesia" we have to start with the introductory mortal courses, experiencing and exploring along the way with the Godly promise that the right way can be found if we are willing to do what is required. This path will require collective comprehension and action, spiritually, emotionally, and physically.

My goal is to put these two questions and others in proper perspective, to provide answers that spiritually resonate with our souls, perhaps providing an "aha" experience relative to where we are now and where we are going.

Why Experience?

And God said, Let us make man in our image, after our likeness: and let them have dominion over the fish of the sea, and over the fowl of the air, and over the cattle, and over all the earth, and over every creeping thing that creepeth upon the earth **(Genesis 1:26, emphasis added).**

Why is experience a foundational component in the process of returning to God's presence? This scripture helps to explain why. Adam, Eve, and all of their family have been given the right and responsibility for the operation of this temporal world. The scripture also implies how humankind is to function. Look at the breadth of experience that will be required from being made in the "image" of God all the way to having "dominion" in this earthly realm.

This second scripture, instruction to Adam and Eve, makes an interesting and revealing pronouncement:

. . . cursed is the ground for thy sake; in sorrow shalt thou eat of it all the days of thy life; thorns also and thistles shall it bring forth to thee; and thou shalt eat the herb of the field; in the sweat of thy face shalt thou eat bread, till thou return unto the ground . . . (Genesis 3:17-19).

It is clear that after Adam and Eve's expulsion from the Garden of Eden that the ground would no longer freely provide the food necessary for life. It is also apparent that without constant manipulation and work through Adam and Eve's efforts, they would not have the necessary life-giving and preserving elements. This became the new mortal mode of operation for all of their posterity.

Nothing has changed in our day—the spirit of that "new condition" is still operable. There can be no misunderstanding that God's plan provides for a broad spectrum of experience including highs and lows, all the while eating our bread as a result of working "in the sweat of thy face."

Do you feel that requiring us to work all of our lives in order to eat and to experience all kinds of events, including pain and sorrow, is a blessing or a cursing (evil or misfortune)? Is this the kind of experience needed for us to return Home (where God dwells)? If it is, then this is not a cursing, but a blessing of eternal magnitude. Adam and Eve embraced it as such and I trust their example. This "complete" experience was ordained from the beginning and can come in no other way.

In D&C 122, for Joseph Smith's benefit and understanding, the Lord detailed a possible number of challenging, even fearful life experiences including:

> *And if thou should be cast into the pit, or into the hands of murderers, and the sentence of death passed upon thee; if thou be cast into the deep; if the billowing surge conspire against thee; if fierce winds become thine enemy; if the heavens gather blackness, and all the elements combine to hedge up the way; and above all, if the very jaws of hell gape open the mouth wide after thee, know thou, my son, that all these things shall give thee experience, and shall be for thy good* (D&C 122:7).

This is a clear clarification of the value of experience and God's attitude toward it.

Can we expect that anything should be different for us? I think not—the practicality of mortal life is that all experience should be for our good. This doesn't mean that we can decide to be rebels and choose sin over righteousness. If we are striving to be faithful children, then all these experiences will be for our good and are necessary for our progress.

All of this makes perfect sense when viewing the "whys" of creation through the lens of "obtaining Eternal Life," or the quality of life that God has. The "body" of experience must be complete, it must include the sublime with the base, the beautiful with the ugly, requiring each of us to make choices between them. Will you be faithful or rebellious? Will you look to the source of Light or the source of Darkness? Will you align your life with God's will or with the world's?

Lehi in speaking to his son, Jacob, said,

> *For it must needs be, that there is an*
> *opposition in all things. If not so . . .*
> *righteousness could not be brought to pass,*
> *neither wickedness, neither holiness nor*
> *misery, neither good nor bad*
> (2 Nephi 2:11).

Eternal Life (God's Life) nor the prospect of choosing it would be possible without these opportunities and experiences. We will not always choose wisely, but we can learn from our poor choices and still gain Eternal Life. This is one of the remarkable blessings of the Atonement, the reconciliation of Gods' children to Him to overcome the consequences of sin, performed by Jesus Christ in the Garden of Gethsemane and on the cross. Experience must include options for choosing for it to have "eternal" value. Choosing instigates growth and ultimately is the qualifier needed for our return Home.

Joseph Smith, the prophet the Lord called to restore His Church (The Church of Jesus Christ of Latter-Day Saints) in 1830, led a party from Kirtland, Ohio to Missouri, bringing clothing and provisions for the embattled saints (modern-day members of Christ's Church) under threat of mob violence. He received a revelation regarding this situation while at Fishing River, Missouri that was recorded as section 105 in the *Doctrine and Covenants*. The instruction in these verses is another testament of the Lord's attitude and instruction about experience.

And my people must needs be chastened until they learn obedience, if it must needs be, by the things which they suffer.

. . . and that my people may be taught more perfectly, and have experience, and know more perfectly concerning their duty, and the things which I require at their hands (D&C 105:6, 10).

There are so many scriptural witnesses, both ancient and modern, that gaining experience is a requirement of God's plan of salvation (being delivered from sin according to the Lord's requirements). We have a responsibility to gain experience and use it wisely, according to the commandments and personal instruction given us by the Spirit (Holy Ghost, a member of the Godhead, comprised of Father-In-Heaven, Jesus Christ, and the Holy Ghost).

But wo unto him that has the law given, yea, that has all the commandments of God, like unto us, and that transgresseth them, and that wasteth the days of his probation, for awful is his state (2 Nephi 9:27)!

I think this scripture is self-explanatory. I don't want to waste my days. It seems to me that there are so many potential counterfeits in the world that may distract us from what is important. That tool or process which when used properly may provide temporal "rewards" and may also inflict devastating harm when overused or used improperly. I have great concern regarding the addictions I perceive to social media, the Internet and technology in general. Those negative outcomes seem to separate us from the things that are really important in life. People are becoming distant and isolated from those around them, letting the ease of technology take the place of needful human development and interaction. All of this world's "tools" must be used with wisdom and self-control.

It is interesting that we have no idea how old we are considering pre-mortal life, but it is safe to surmise that it is was far longer than life here on earth. Yet, it is this short mortal period that becomes the deciding factor on what happens after mortality. That is how important experience is and what we do with it.

The Lord has made it very clear that experience is vital in earth life and in preparation for Eternal Life, the life that God enjoys. Now, it is our responsibility to learn from our decisions and experiences to make our lives continually progressive in becoming worthy to return His Home. Even sins and rebellion can be progressive if we are willing to learn, repent, and align our lives with God's will.

In the development of the human embryo, the heart develops before the brain and plays a significant role in brain development. The significance of this relationship does not disappear after birth. According to the Institute of HeartMath, "The heart and brain maintain a continuous two-way dialogue, each influencing the other's functioning. The signals the heart sends to the brain can influence perception, emotional processing, and higher cognitive functions. This system and circuitry is viewed by neurocardiology researchers as a 'heart brain.'"

I don't think it is a coincidence that in spiritual terms we are counseled to listen to our hearts to confirm truth and that there is a "physical" application of this process with the heart's influence on perception, emotional processing and higher cognitive functions. Our bodies have a Godly design for the practical use, progressive development, and aligning of innumerable experiences to meet the eternal requirements for our return Home, respecting our singular uniqueness.

What is the value of memory? In a real way we become who we are because of our experiences and the lingering power of memories. They can fill heart and mind. They are motivational, inspiring movement, either toward darkness or light. We often turn to them when chaos, confusion, or emptiness affects our lives. If they have a foundation in truth, the Spirit can use them in providing comfort, instruction, and motivation to discover who we are, where we ought to go, and provide the incentive and energy to keep progressing.

Times of frustration and depression are not foreign to me. During these periods, I have questioned my relationship with God and whether or not Heavenly help will come. My automatic response, as I'm trying to make sense of things, is to review memories of strength and help given at other times in my life. These become second witnesses of God's love and willingness to give aid. The memories provide emotional and spiritual strength to keep me going. I am able to better exercise faith and trust, because of them.

Some years ago, my wife and I were at the Conference Center in Salt Lake City for a session of General Conference. When President Gordon B. Hinkley entered, all the congregation stood. He reached his seat and those on the stand sat down. However, the congregation kept standing and without prompting the strains of the hymn "We Thank Thee, O God, for a Prophet" could be heard, first as a quiet background to the moment, then within a few seconds as a full-throated anthem. Everyone in the congregation bore testimony of the calling of this prophet and rejoiced in that testimony through this sacred hymn. President Hinkley stood again, followed by all those on the stand.

I know this hymn well. It is one of my favorites. I tried to sing, but was so filled with the Spirit that my physical response was a constriction in my throat that wouldn't permit the words to leave my lips. My spirit soared in the attempt to bear witness through this music. I wept as that heavenly chorus seemed to raise the whole assembly beyond this telestial realm. The chorus ended, but the memory lives on, bringing me to tears whenever I ponder upon it.

Truth and light (enlightenment and ennobling influence given to all of Father's children from Christ) filled me that day and those heavenly embers have never gone out. I hope you have had that kind of experience in your life, a light turned on through memory to illuminate your way forward while banishing darkness.

Whenever I have deeply troubling challenges that might cause me to lose sight of who I am and why I am on the earth, my heart and mind replay this and other sacred memories. The result is increased strength and will, propelling me forward to exercise faith and trust that Father will get me where I need to be. There is a condition—I must keep striving.

Heart and mind, spirit and body, everything is in place for us to have the experiences we need to prepare us to return Home, always conditional upon the choices we make. This is truly a process and not an event.

My career or the seeming lack of one at times has been a bane in my life, a trial that has been continuous from about age 25 to the present, with only short "vacations" along the way. Following college, I chose an initial career path in business that it appears I never had any true affinity or natural ability for, as I look back upon it.

I spent a number of years as a financial and investment advisor. I remember with painful clarity and thanksgiving (Are these at odds with each other?) a situation that arose where our little company was under threat of a lawsuit for an investment that went bad. We were not at fault with the investment, but the cost of a legal defense was far more than our ability to pay.

I remember going to Temple Square in Salt Lake City (the land and buildings surrounding the Salt Lake Temple) and sitting by one of the fountains, pouring out my fearful heart to our Father. I did not receive a Heavenly intervention as I had hoped at that time, but without any spiritual fanfare we were able to negotiate a resolve that I'm certain was influenced by a gift of understanding, perhaps to both parties, permitting the resolve to be acceptable.

The churning of emotions and the ever-present knot in the pit of my stomach were real and have provided some wisdom that is not forgotten when viewing this experience in the light of God's blessing and the "quiet help" I received. Both memories are of great value, providing valuable support for later life and work decisions.

I am so thankful for life experiences that have tested me and for the Heavenly support that has always been available, if I sought it, and for the ability to relive these empowering experiences through memory. Memories are an incredibly valuable tool in aligning my life with God's will.

New experiences can invite exploration, introspection, even fear, and certainly require decision-making. A valuable relationship exists between choices, experiences, memories, and decisions to be made in life. There is a tangible link, a thread that binds these together as a benefit, if we will use it—that link is faith.

In January of 1833, Joseph Smith began the School of the Prophets in a small room above the Newel K. Whitney store in Kirtland, Ohio. In that sacred space the leaders of the Church were instructed in many topics relative to the establishment of God's kingdom now upon the earth. In a revelation preparatory to the founding of the school, the Lord said:

> *And as all have not faith, seek ye diligently and teach one another words of wisdom; yea, seek ye out of the best books words of wisdom; seek learning, even by study and also by faith* (D&C 88:118).

For three years, my wife and I served a Church Service Mission within the BYU-Idaho Pathway Program. We mentored students of all ages, backgrounds, and ethnicity in this college preparation program, helping them to meet the requirements pursuant to obtaining a college degree.

At the assembly of each new student cohort, we had the challenge of helping the students come to know that they can gain college level experience and knowledge by study and faith. For some, being in the program was an act of faith, overcoming the fear of failure, of not being "college material." We witnessed students learning math by faith, when the very subject terrified them and they were certain that they could not successfully master it.

They came to understand that all knowledge, not just spiritual knowledge, can be learned by faith. Perhaps that is how all knowledge is ultimately learned. These experiences changed them and the trajectory of their lives. Experience, based upon the exercise of faith is transforming.

Eternal Life and Saviors

*For behold this is my work and my
glory, to bring to pass the immortality
and eternal life of man*
(Moses 1:39, emphasis added).

Not so long ago, I thought, maybe guessed is a better verb, that immortality and eternal life were basically describing the same condition, perhaps with a small nuance of difference. But, this is not so. Immortality is a free gift of life without death or in other words, we live forever—it is hard to comprehend that isn't it? In mortality, everything has a beginning and an end, but once we are resurrected, we will not suffer physical death again, never to have our spirit and body separated.

Eternal life sounds like the same thing, because eternal means: everlasting, undying, perpetual. However, the sheer number of times the phrase "immortality and eternal life" is used in the scriptures conveys an understanding that they are not the same, that the scripture language is not just being redundant.

The prophet Enos, at the end of his written record in the Book of Mormon, described what it will be like to receive eternal life.

> *And I soon go to the place of my rest, which is with my Redeemer; for I know that in him I shall rest. And I rejoice in the day when my mortal shall put on immortality, and shall stand before him; then shall I see his face with pleasure, and he will say unto me: Come unto me, ye blessed, there is a place prepared for you in the mansions of my Father* (Enos 1:27).

"Eternal" is a descriptive word, describing the kind of life God lives and desires to provide for each of us, if we are willing to receive it. Try imagining what it would be like to be in God's presence, living with him, being surrounded by everything of a celestial nature, feeling, seeing, embracing, and belonging there. This is far beyond my ability.

It is obvious from the scriptures that those who have been given the opportunity to glimpse that world couldn't find words to describe it or the people who inhabit it. This statement of Joseph Smith's regarding seeing the Savior in the Kirtland Temple is one such example of the challenge of our language to adequately depict celestial glory.

> *The veil was taken from our minds, and the eyes of our understanding were opened.*
>
> *We saw the Lord standing upon the breastwork of the pulpit, before us; and under his feet was a paved work of pure gold, in color like amber.*
>
> *His eyes were as a flame of fire; the hair of his head was white like the pure snow; his countenance shone above the brightness of the sun; and his voice was as the sound of the rushing of great waters, even the voice of Jehovah, . . .* (D&C 110:1-3).

Breathtaking, yet I sense our language has limited ability even for Joseph!

It is vital for us to come to realize what the process is of becoming worthy and able to receive Eternal Life. Consider the Apostle Paul's words, as he expressed his witness that Jesus Christ is a "priest forever after the order of Melchisedec." He said,

> *Though he were a Son, yet learned he obedience by the things which he suffered; and being made perfect, he became the author of eternal salvation unto all them that obey him; called of God an high priest after the order of Melchisedec* (Hebrews 5:8-10).

Please note that Jesus Christ learned obedience "by the things which he suffered," by "ennobling experiences," which are very important in the focus of this discussion. He also "became the author of eternal salvation unto all them that obey him." The term "eternal salvation" is so important, because receiving immortality does not mean that we have experienced salvation. "Eternal salvation" certainly implies that we are saved in a state of Eternal Life or the quality of life one has who lives with God.

We all must be "elevated" or ennobled in order to leave this telestial world and to be invited into a celestial existence. Our "mortal course" with its primitive language, thoughts, and attitudes must be purified and raised to a level beyond our current comprehension. Desire, righteous desire, must progress to belief, then faith, and after the trial of our faith to knowledge. Having knowledge is the promise the Savior has made if we will align our lives with God's will.

> *It is impossible for a man to be saved in ignorance* (D&C 131:6).

> *Whatever principle of intelligence we attain unto in this life, it will rise with us in the resurrection.*

> *And if a person gains more knowledge and intelligence in this life through his diligence and obedience than another, he will have so much the advantage in the world to come* (D&C 130:18-19).

> *As well might man stretch forth his puny arm to stop the Missouri river in its decreed course, or to turn it up stream, as to hinder the Almighty from pouring down knowledge from heaven upon the heads of the Latter-day Saints* (D&C 121:33).

This transformation is not possible unless we desire it and are willing to do as the Savior commands. In a practical, everyday sense what is required?

Nephi and Lehi's vision of the Tree of Life (1 Nephi 8:10-35 in the Book of Mormon) provides a very pictorial representation. In my mind, my inner vision, I can see God's children on that "strait and narrow path," people of all descriptions, some crippled, bent over, others blind or deaf, some holding the hands of others who have grasped the iron rod (the gospel and word of Christ), unable to do it on their own. There are those that appear as if their life's journey has been easy and others look to be worn out, barely moving forward on the path, yet all striving to progress toward the "love of God" and Eternal Life.

Their souls have been enriched by life experiences and are filled with memories, perhaps diverse from the people around them, but necessary for their growth, motivating them to start up the path. They are propelled forward by the soul-stretching and refinement that life has encouraged, no matter how slow the journey. Speed is unimportant. What is important is staying focused on the Tree of Life (Christ and the love of God), the source of light and joy and keeping hold of eternal truths, trusting God to get them where they need to be.

Endurance is a fundamental component of this journey. Some give up, others are tempted away, fooled by the "spirit of the world" to turn from the source of joy to one seemingly clothed in ease, pleasure, and the gifts of the world. Whatever has enticed them to turn from the source of light—how sad it is, for they may never know what it is they are missing until it might be too late.

Consider this excerpt from Nephi's discussion with his brothers after he was permitted to see the same vision his father received.

> *(Tree of Life) whose fruit is most precious*
> *and most desirable above all other fruits;*
> *yea, and it is the greatest of all the gifts of*
> *God* (1 Nephi 15:36).

A more modern witness is found in D&C 14:7.

> *And, if you keep my commandments*
> *and endure to the end you shall have*
> *eternal life, which gift is the greatest of all*
> *the gifts of God.*

The practical side of preparing to go Home and enjoy the quality of life that is God's life has some real challenges. Let's ponder on this experience when a young man came to Jesus with an important question.

And, behold, one came and said unto him, Good Master, what good thing shall I do, that I may have eternal life?

And he said unto him, Why callest thou me good? there is none good but one, that is, God: but if thou wilt enter into life, keep the commandments.

He saith unto him, Which? Jesus said, Thou shalt do no murder, Thou shalt not commit adultery, Thou shalt not steal, Thou shalt not bear false witness, Honour thy father and thy mother: and, Thou shalt love thy neighbor as thyself.

The young man saith unto him, All these things have I kept from my youth up: what lack I yet?

Jesus said unto him, If thou wilt be perfect, go and sell that thou hast, and give to the poor, and thou shalt have treasure in heaven: and come and follow me.

But when the young man heard that saying, he went away sorrowful: for he had great possessions (Matthew 19:16-22).

It is important to understand how difficult it can be to recognize and "embrace ennobling experiences." It is through the Spirit that we will gain the comprehension needed regarding our experiences and hopefully, we will not reject them as this young man did. However, I have found that when enveloped in stress and pain, it can be very difficult for a person to feel the Spirit.

The Lord has given a commandment that I have personally discovered invites the Spirit, even under very difficult circumstances.

Thou shalt thank the Lord thy God in
all things. (D&C 59:7)

When I am struggling, trying to feel the Spirit, if I genuinely thank our Father for his tender care, (no matter what difficulty is going on for I can always recognize many blessings and tender mercies), the Spirit always comes. With the companionship of the Holy Ghost, we will understand the nature of the experience we are having and how we should respond.

Jesus went on to have a discussion with His disciples about the challenges of being rich with earthly goods and being able to "enter into the kingdom of heaven." There appears to me to be an additional lesson in this experience about obtaining Eternal Life.

Jesus first answered the young man's question with instruction to "keep the commandments." That is what I would expect to be instructed in, if I had asked the question. These specific commandments given by the Savior contain the "core" responsibilities of all commandments pertaining to our earthly relationships with others. To say it another way, our performances in life must contain these principles and we must internalize the spirit that attends them.

The young man said that he was faithful in keeping all of the stated commandments. The Son of God then gave instruction of a higher spiritual level necessary to obtain eternal life, inviting the young man to follow Him. I believe this was about being a committed follower, a disciple – certainly, and more. This was an invitation to offer the gift of his life in similitude of the Savior's—to love his neighbors and to take upon himself the burdens of others, even as the Savior does, to become a "savior" himself.

This higher spiritual level or requirement seems to be embodied in a scripture given to the prophet, Joseph Smith. On February 24, 1834, Joseph received a revelation that explained why the Lord allowed the saints in Jackson County to be persecuted.

But inasmuch as they keep not my commandments, and hearken not to observe all my words, the kingdoms of the world shall prevail against them. For they were set to be a light unto the world, and to be the saviors of men;

And inasmuch as they are not the saviors of men, they are as salt that has lost its savor, and is thenceforth good for nothing but to be cast out and trodden under foot of men. (D&C 103:8-10)

Here again, we find the instruction to keep the commandments, including observing all of God's words. The commandments are written in the scriptures and hopefully in our hearts. Where are we to find "all of God's words?" Consider all of the "authorized sources" of God's instructions, including: the current Prophet, First Presidency, Apostles, and other general authorities and their instructional sources. In this day and age, those sources are easy to find.

There is another source that is absolutely vital for our understanding and performance—the Gift of the Holy Ghost. Personal revelation is essential in order to keep the commandments and observe all of God's words. Oliver Cowdery was instructed in April of 1829 by direct revelation through Joseph Smith:

Yea, behold, I will tell you in your mind and in your heart, by the Holy Ghost, which shall come upon you and which shall dwell in your heart.

Now, behold, this is the spirit of revelation; behold, this is the spirit by which Moses brought the children of Israel through the Red Sea on dry ground (D&C 8:2-3).

This promise to Oliver is also the assurance each of us has that we can know exactly what God wants us to do in applying the commandments and all of God's words to our lives. This is how we will complete the life mission we each have. We must be willing to not only receive, but to do. To be with God and enjoy the quality of life He has, there is much for us to learn, embrace and do while here in mortality.

It has become clear to me that God's "plan of salvation" was designed for all of us to be saviors. Here is what Elder John A. Widtsoe of the Quorum of the Twelve Apostles had to say:

"In our preexistent state, in the day of the great council, we made a certain agreement with the Almighty. The Lord proposed a plan, conceived by him. We accepted it. Since the plan is intended for all men, we become parties to the salvation of every person under the plan. We agreed, right then and there, to be not only saviors for ourselves, but . . . Saviors for the whole human family. We went into a partnership with the Lord. The working out of the plan became then not merely the Father's work, and the Savior's work, but also our work. The least of us, the humblest, is in partnership with the Almighty in achieving the purpose of the eternal plan of salvation" ("The Worth of Souls," Utah Genealogical and Historical Magazine, Oct. 1934, 189).

The practical application of being a savior has been taught by God's authorized servants throughout human history. The prophet, Alma, when instructing at the waters of Mormon, prior to the baptism of a number of those who knew his words to be true, said this about conversion, godly service, and baptism:

> *Behold, here are the waters of Mormon (for thus were they called) and now, as ye are desirous to come into the fold of God, and to be called his people, and are willing to bear one another's burdens, that they may be light;*
>
> *Yea, and are willing to mourn with those that mourn; yea, and comfort those that stand in need of comfort, and to stand as witnesses of God at all times and in all things, and in all places that ye may be in, even until death, that ye may be redeemed*

of God, and be numbered with those of the first resurrection, that ye may have eternal life—

Now I say unto you, if this be the desire of your hearts, what have you against being baptized in the name of the Lord, as a witness before him that ye have entered into a covenant with him, that ye will serve him and keep his commandments, that he may pour out his Spirit more abundantly upon you (Mosiah 18:8-10)?

Is this not an invitation to become the saviors that we all covenanted to be in pre-mortality? Isn't this a great example of the practical application of this covenant to serve and lift the burdens of others in similitude of Jesus Christ's fulfilled covenant, loving as He loves?

We take upon ourselves the yoke of discipleship and charity (the pure love of Christ) upon accepting baptism into the Savior's Church. I suppose that in substance, this mirrors what we agreed to do before leaving our Father's home in pre-mortally. We then are covenant partners with the Father and the Savior in their work to "bring to pass the immortality and eternal life of man." Our commission to be saviors is real. This is our work!

The Refining Power of the Spirit

And the Spirit giveth light to every man that cometh into the world; and the Spirit enlighteneth every man through the world, that hearkeneth to the voice of the Spirit.

And every one that hearkeneth to the voice of the Spirit cometh unto God, even the Father
(D&C 84:46-47, emphasis added).

Experiences become ennobling through our responses to them and the refining blessings of the Spirit. Often, we are guided into experiences in order to receive the education needed to strengthen a weakness or open a new vista. Oftentimes they can be very challenging, requiring significant adjustments in our attitudes and focus, all the while giving opportunity to embrace, learn, and use these God-given gifts.

The Spirit has responsibility for the giving of gifts to all of God's children. The Spirit will also instruct in how to use them. The scriptures make it clear that each of us has received at least one gift, maybe more. Consider this instruction given to Joseph Smith.

To some it is given by the Holy Ghost to know that Jesus Christ is the Son of God, and that he was crucified for the sins of the world.

To others it is given to believe on their words, that they also might have eternal life if they continue faithful . . .

And again, verily I say unto you, to some is given, by the Spirit of God, the word of wisdom.

To another is given the word of knowledge, that all may be taught to be wise and to have knowledge.

And again, to some it is given to have faith to be healed;

And to others it is given to have faith to heal.

And again, to some is given the working of miracles;

And to others it is given to prophesy;

And to others the discerning of spirits.

And again, it is given to some to speak with tongues;

And to another is given the interpretation of tongues.

And all these gifts come from God, for the benefit of the children of God (D&C 46:13-14, 17-26).

The prophet Moroni, in giving instruction regarding the gifts of God, recorded this witness as found in the Book of Mormon:

And again, I exhort you, my brethren, that ye deny not the gifts of God, for they are many; and they come from the same God. And there are different ways that these gifts are administered; but it is the same God who worketh all in all; and they are given by the manifestations of the

Spirit of God unto men, to profit them.
(Moroni 10:8)

All of God's gifts and all of the ministering of the Spirit are given to bless God's children to prepare them to return Home and to participate in His work on the way. The witnesses of prophets and others leave no doubt as to God's desire for His children and the purpose of mortal life. Every experience in life, the good and the bad, as we might view them, have the potential to be ennobling if we permit the Spirit to work within us.

It is my experience that contact with the Spirit, not just with the gifts listed, but especially constant contact has a refining impact upon the souls of all men and women. The Spirit encourages and inspires Godly change in the individual that can be seen in the way we speak, dress, and interact with others. Coarse language morphs into words and phrases that are "higher" in their tone, descriptive power, and meaning. Men and women speak in the language the Spirit inspires, instead of the gross and crass language inspired by the world.

Kindness and respect with a desire to bless influences our interactions with others. Selfishness becomes service. We begin to think, plan, and act differently. We no longer turn to the world to fill our time and desires. We become more centered on helping others and less devoted to self-service and pride. God's children move from pessimism to optimism.

We even change our surroundings, making certain they are clean and orderly in response to the Spirit's refining influence. We no longer are comfortable visiting places where the Spirit will not be found.

All things designed for the blessing of God's children are in His hands. We come to understand that the greatest blessings in life, the greatest happiness and joy, and the most fulfillment come when aligned with God's will for us, instead of pridefully trying to go our own way. Nevertheless, we get to choose, not only that we must choose. No choice is in reality a choice.

Association with the Spirit will begin to change our desires. We will begin to understand the reality and process of becoming one with

God. As this takes place, won't we begin to think more like our Father, make decisions like Him, and act like Him? I believe we will.

Blessing or Punishment?

. . . for I do know that whosoever shall put their trust in God shall be supported in their trials, and their troubles, and their afflictions, and shall be lifted up at the last da.
(Alma 36:3, emphasis added).

I recognize that this scripture has several component connections, such as obedience and faith. However, I want to focus on the kinds of experience detailed here: "trials, troubles, and afflictions." It appears that exercising "trust in God" does not prompt from God a promise that we will not have those troubling experiences. Yet, that is how we want to be treated, a very "mortal" desire, I suppose. The promise given is that we will be "supported" through these experiences until we are "lifted up at the last day."

This bears a powerful witness that experiences, even difficult challenges, are a requirement of our existence. I have finally come to know that even the most uncomfortable of experiences are a necessary part of my life—part of the preparation to be "lifted up at the last day."

I'm certain that you can look back on your life as I have and recount, even relive, a number of very challenging and painful experiences, remembering the powerful emotions that may have tested your resolve and testimony. At the time of each one, you may have wondered "why me?" When no resolve was imminent, did the silent pleading of your heart ask, "Lord, why won't you help me?" fearing that there would be no answer?

As much as we wish it were different, we probably make the most valuable changes in our lives as a result of the pain we are required to experience and oftentimes endure. We learn more through our efforts to resolve pain than we do in peace. As a result, this experiential process naturally leads us to God's doorstep. If we knock with a genuine desire for His help, willing to follow His counsel, He will answer and we will come to know Him. Relief will come and we will receive a gift through the process that is beyond all earthy value—to know God, that He lives, loves us, and we can trust Him to provide for our needs.

Now, with this understanding in place the question we ought to ask when challenge and pain come calling is "why not me!" God will manifest Himself in the resolve.

Who of God's children can definitively determine what preparatory experiences they need in order to return Home? No one! We would love to choose our experiences and the outcomes, but Father knows what we need with exactness. We make decisions, some are as Father would have, some are not. We make mistakes. We commit sins. In a way, all are progressive, if we learn from them and strive to follow the Light that will come.

We don't see ourselves as God sees us. Hard things happen to us and we wonder if we are being punished. The scriptures are clear about receiving punishment for sin. Perhaps this provides the simplest type of understanding of why we shouldn't commit sin.

I have another way of looking at it, at punishment. I believe that our Father is a merciful god. If punishments are given, in reality they are simply the experiences that we need for our education, conversion, and progression. Since all of God's children have been given the "Light of Christ," (although, some may not be willing to receive it) and since I have been given this gift and still make bad decisions, commit sins, making me unworthy to be in God's presence, it is obvious I need different experiences that will get my attention. Call them punishment if you will, but I prefer to see them as tender mercies, blessings that I need to encourage repentance and ongoing striving to do right.

Looking back on our own individual history, we can begin to appreciate the gifts of the "Light of Christ" and the "Gift of the Holy Ghost." Sadly, spiritual laziness is an unfortunate reality. Incentives, promptings, and pokes are often required to restart us or keep us moving along the right path. Blessings or punishments, whatever you call them, I need them.

Do You Trust God?

O Lord, I have trusted in thee,
and I will trust in thee forever
(2 Nephi 4:34, emphasis added).

I have a story to tell. Let me give you a little background. I lost my job as a business skills trainer, a consequence of the economic downturn that had been developing for some time. Essentially, I had been out of work for six years, only able to pick up some occasional labor now and again as I tried to find work utilizing my background. My wife was supporting our family with only a little help from me. At this stage of life, this wasn't supposed to be happening.

My wife and I were traveling with another couple in the back seat of their pickup truck. As we visited, the discussion turned to travel and other opportunities friends were enjoying, because of their financial abilities. I was hurting. It didn't take very long for me to emotionally withdraw from the conversation, wishing I could transport myself almost anywhere else. I attempted to get lost in the scenery that was continually changing as we travelled down the freeway. Try as I might, I was still there, unable to stop hearing what was being said. My reflection on the window looked back at me, eyes and face painted with the broad brush of pain.

It is hard to describe what I was feeling. In the scriptures, the Savior describes His pain as "exquisite." I have learned that this word also means acute or intense, not just beautiful or delicate. I don't mean to imply that my pain was in any way similar to what the Savior experienced, only that in my current mortal condition, that is how it felt, very intense distress.

I hurt with a deep emotional pain, the type that causes you to wonder if you will ever feel good again. I'm certain some of it was pride, some the anguish over my failure to be a provider, and some the self-accusation of career decisions going back many years. I felt shame, failure, and declining self-confidence. This was a pretty depressing emotional package and it was mine.

As I rode along, my stomach in knots, filled with the desire to disappear, the Spirit spoke to me, much to my surprise. (I obviously wasn't in a good place, so this was truly a "tender mercy.") This was more than an impression. The message was very clear. A question was asked that needed to be answered; *Don't you trust me to get you where you need to be?* At first, I was awed by the question and then by the Spirit's powerful touch as mind and heart united in trying to honestly give a response.

As I pondered, my attention was now completely upon the answer. I realized I couldn't say with conviction that I trusted Father to take care of me. I had been cultivating ideas about what my life should be like for quite some time. It became clear that in my prayers I had been trying to "influence" God to turn things the way I wanted them to go. Oftentimes what I think I want isn't what I need. Father already knows what my real needs are. Prayer is the personal, spiritual communication designed for us to come to know God's will for us and to align our wills with His.

I read the records often of blessings given me by those ordained brethren with Priesthood authority to lay hands on my head and speak as the Spirit prompted them. I prayed continually about my life situations. In addition, I had received Priesthood blessings that seemed to provide instruction regarding what was in front of me at this time. I thought I understood what was said in the blessings and what ought to happen next, but as it turned out, I didn't understand. I discovered that in setting my "preconceptions" aside, the instruction in the blessings could mean something different. Now, with this "direct spiritual inquiry" in front of me, I recognized, over time, that the Lord had something very different in mind for me.

I had a couple of pathways that I believed were good and either could play a significant part in the completion of my life's mission. I thought I had "spiritual evidence" that one of them should be the path to be followed. Serving a full-time mission for the Church of Jesus Christ of Latter-Day Saints in proselyting or any other service my wife and I could perform was a part of my "hoped for plan." I came to know I was mistaken.

Father had other plans for me—service opportunities I could not foresee, a "mission" within our family and work as an academic advisor for Salt Lake Community College. My wife and I had already served a Church Service Mission for three years in the "Pathway Program" designed to help people around the world get the college level education that would bless their lives. In addition, we each served in the Draper Temple, helping to provide the ordinances needed for all of God's children to be prepared in order to return Home.

This experience with the Spirit was an important steppingstone for me to realize the Lord wanted me to follow a different path. For the record, I am not disappointed that my earlier intentions did not work out. I have been filled with a tremendous sense of thanksgiving that I am doing what the Lord wants me to do with family, church, and work stewardships. This is a gift of the Spirit available to all of God's children who align their lives with His will. We don't have to be perfect in it, just striving.

In what has been referred to as the "Psalm of Nephi" in The Book of Mormon these heartfelt expressions of Nephi's have also touched me and in terms of my life experiences, accurately describe my feelings.

> *Behold, my soul delighteth in the things of the Lord; and my heart pondereth continually upon the things which I have seen and heard.*

> *Nevertheless, notwithstanding the great goodness of the Lord, in showing me his great and marvelous works, my heart exclaimeth: O wretched man that I am! Yea, my heart sorroweth because of my flesh; my soul grieveth because of mine iniquities.*

I am encompassed about, because of the temptations and the sins which do so easily beset me.

And when I desire to rejoice, my heart groaneth because of my sins; nevertheless, I know in whom I have trusted.
(2 Nephi 4:16-19)

The prophet Mormon made this comment as recorded in the Book of Mormon while writing about Alma and his followers escaping from King Noah and settling in the land of Helam:

Nevertheless the Lord seeth fit to chasten his people; yea, he trieth their patience and their faith. Nevertheless—whosoever putteth his trust in him the same shall be lifted up at the last day
(Mosiah 23:21-22).

Alma and his people were able to settle this land in peace for only a short time. They were soon brought into bondage by an army of the Lamanites and suffered in very difficult circumstances. That history was in front of Mormon as he made this comment, knowing what these people were required to endure. He knew of the miracle that later provided for their release and that if we trust the Lord we will be "lifted up at the last day," whatever and whenever that is for each of us.

I don't think this necessarily means the end of our days. Being "lifted up at the last day" may occur a number of times in our lives as we struggle and strive through difficult challenges. When things get hard and troubles mount up with no end in sight, I have come to know that if I persevere in trusting the Lord, relief and blessings come and I am a better man because of what I have experienced—the pain, the effort, and the joy.

Alma the Younger, after resigning his position as chief judge of the land, began a "missionary journey" throughout all the Nephite lands as High Priest, first in Zarahemla. He asked these questions of the members of the church:

> *. . . have ye spiritually been born of*
> *God? Have ye received his image in your*
> *countenances? Have ye experienced this*
> *mighty change in your hearts?*
> (Alma 5:14)

I am going to start with the last question first. What is the "mighty change" of heart he is speaking of? It is when we receive the word of God and accept it, believe it, and "own" it sufficiently to change our hearts, desires, and how we think and act.

The second question easily refers to being filled with light and truth.

> *. . . and whatsoever is light is Spirit, even*
> *the Spirit of Jesus Christ.* (D&C 84:45)

Is your expectation the same as mine, that being filled with the Spirit of Jesus Christ will place His image in our countenances? I bear testimony it will. I have seen it in many faithful people. That image is visible even to human sight.

Now to the first question, to be "spiritually born of God." When Alma the Younger recovered from an angelic visitation, after being unable to speak and having no strength in his limbs for three days and three nights, he said,

> *. . . I have repented of my sins, and have*
> *been redeemed of the Lord; behold I am*
> *born of the Spirit.*
>
> *And the Lord said unto me: Marvel not*
> *that all mankind, yea, men and women,*
> *all nations, kindreds, tongues and people,*
> *must be born again; yea, born of God,*
> *changed from their carnal and fallen state,*
> *to a state of righteousness, being redeemed*
> *of God, becoming his sons and daughters;*
>
> *And thus they become new creatures;*
> *and unless they do this, then can in nowise*

inherit the kingdom of God
(Mosiah 27:24-26).

To be spiritually born of God means that through repentance we will be changed from our "carnal and fallen state to a state of righteousness." We know that by being obedient to God's commands we will be blessed with Eternal Life through the Atonement of the Savior.

We are spiritual sons and daughters of God. However, to be able to return Home and take our place as His redeemed children, we must become "new creatures" or new people by overcoming the attractions and temptations of the world. This is done by being born of the Spirit, having our souls cleansed and purified by the Holy Ghost. That can only be done by aligning our wills with our Father's. We must listen to the Spirit and obey. Perfection is not possible here, but striving to progress is.

Trusting God provides the personal wisdom and energy needed to make all of life's experiences ultimately ennobling, just as Alma the Younger's were.

Obedience

And my people must needs be chastened until they learn obedience, if it must needs be by the things which they suffer
(D&C 105:6, emphasis added).

With the understanding that choices come in various levels of "quality" or value, what influences your decision-making? Since making choices is a key component of life and a vital purpose for mortality, what do your choices reveal about you?

As we grow and mature, most of us, from the time we were toddlers, fought to make our own choices. With hundreds of decisions being made each day by you, let's talk about them. Setting aside the easy ones like what to wear, what to eat, and those that are similar, what are the most powerful influences in your decision-making? How do you judge what to do with decisions that will impact the quality of your life, perhaps for years? Do you have a guide for making them?

Every child of God came to the earth having been given an internal guide, the Light of Christ, to provide Heavenly assistance with choice making. We refer to it as our "conscience," but it is literally the Light of Christ or Christ's spirit as we have learned from scripture (D&C84:45). As with all Heavenly Influences, we can choose to follow or ignore.

Whatever our decision, we must realize that consequences will follow (remember, doing nothing is a choice) either improving our opportunities for the future or inviting ruin as described by the scriptures.

On January 2, 1831, the Lord said to Joseph Smith:

. . . if ye are prepared ye shall not fear
(D&C 38:30).

To be prepared is to be obedient. True "preparation" requires efforts that are both temporal and spiritual in focus. If we are God's children and He loves us, why do we struggle to follow Him, to prepare according to His instructions? Is it anger, pride, confusion or rebellion? I suppose it could be many things, but getting over it is a vital step in our progression.

These next thoughts are the result of my life experience, influenced by insufficient attempts to be obedient, but with a desire to reorder my life.

- Obedience is required, because what we are asked to do is what God does. Being His children, it ought to be natural for us to strive to be like Him.
- The only way to enjoy God's Life is to be worthy to be with God and that means to be clean, to be free from the stains of sin. (We can't do that on our own.)
- Being obedient eliminates fear, because God can be trusted. He has blessings, held in reserve, for each of His children that will be given on condition of obedience.
- By being obedient, we begin to see and understand life and its purpose according to Father's design, filling us with confidence and faith.

Mormon, in a letter to his son, Moroni, said:

. . . I fear not what man can do; for perfect love casteth out all fear.

Then, identifying what "perfect love" is he said:

And I am filled with charity, which is everlasting love. (Moroni 8:16-17)

Moroni then adds some additional understanding:

But charity is the pure love of Christ, and it endureth forever; and whoso is

*found possessed of it at the last day, it shall
be well with him.* (Moroni 7:47)

Love, perfect love, charity, everlasting love, "the pure love of Christ" – each of these points to and is a part of the character of Jesus Christ. In all the scriptural descriptions of these qualities there is an implied invitation for us to desire them, seek them, and use them, thus becoming one with Jesus Christ in obedience and the exercise of agency.

There is no room for fear in the heart of the person who is full of faith. This person is obedient, because he or she recognizes that the greatest of all the gifts of God come through obedience, becoming "one with Jesus Christ."

Sin, Repentance, Forgiveness

For the word of the Lord is truth, and whatsoever is truth is light, and whatsoever is light is Spirit, even the Spirit of Jesus Christ (**D&C 84:45, emphasis added**).

There is only one source of light, Jesus Christ the Savior. He is the source of all truth, redemptive power, physical and spiritual light. This scripture makes the Savior's central position in the Plan of Salvation and its earthly operation abundantly clear.

It is interesting that our name for the star that provides earthly light and warmth is the "sun" and the Savior, the Son, is named as the creator, the organizer of this world. An interesting coincidence? I hope your heart shouts with acclamation as mine does that:

> *. . . there is none other name under heaven given among men, whereby we must be saved.* (Acts 4:12)

> *And the Spirit giveth light to every man that cometh into the world; and the Spirit enlighteneth every man through the world, that hearkeneth to the voice of the Spirit.*

> *And every one that hearkenth to the voice of the Spirit cometh unto God, even the Father.* (D&C 84:46-47)

Each of God's children have Christ's spirit given to them when they come into the world to provide the spiritual light needed to begin the journey and to guide them throughout. Isn't this a gift without equal, without measure?

With this as a background, we need to understand what sin is, because it should be obvious that sin has no light. By definition sin is an immoral act, a transgression against divine law. Sin makes us spiritually unclean and we know that according to this instruction given by the Savior that:

> . . . *no unclean thing can enter into his*
> *(God's)kingdom; . . .* (3 Nephi 27:19)

So, here is an intriguing question. Can sin be ennobling? It certainly does not qualify, at least not on its own. Unrepentant sin poisons the soul, turning the person's focus from light and truth to darkness and untruth. However, within the process of repentance, sin is an element that can provide educational experience, now to be used for our blessing instead of a cursing. That doesn't mean that we should look to sin. To do so offends the Holy Ghost and we risk losing His companionship and influence, a tragedy that can have eternal consequences and tragedy, drawing us away from Jesus Christ.

Our Father knew that each of us would sin and provided a pathway that sin can be used for our progression, to be a component of an ennobling experience.

The Savior in 3 Nephi 27:19 continues with this instruction:

> . . . *therefore nothing entereth into his*
> *(God's) rest save it be those who have*
> *washed their garments in my blood,*
> *because of their faith, and the repentance*
> *of all their sins, and their faithfulness unto*
> *the end.*

This fact should not encourage us to sin, but provides comfort regarding the reality of sin and the "eternal life" antidotes of faith and repentance.

The process of repentance is designed to prepare us to receive forgiveness.

*Behold, he who has repented of his
sins, the same is forgiven, and I the Lord,
remember them no more* (D&C 58:42).

I know the relief, the peace, the sense of cleansing that comes when repentance has been sought, approved and forgiveness has been given. We come to know the kindness and mercy of God in a very personal way, to know that He loves us and is faithful in all His words.

This is such an intimate and individual experience to know that God is aware of me and wants to bless me with all the blessings available for His children. He is no respecter of persons and makes these blessings available for everyone who repents.

There is another aspect of forgiveness that is vital to our progression and cannot be ignored. Consider this instruction:

*Wherefore, I say unto you, that ye
ought to forgive one another; for he that
forgiveth not his brother his trespasses
standeth condemned before the Lord; for
there remaineth in him the greater sin. I,
the Lord, will forgive whom I will forgive,
but of you it is required to forgive all men*
(D&C 64:9-10).

If you have ever felt betrayed or wronged by someone, this can be a very difficult, but obviously a necessary exercise and experience. I have a personal example that stands out in my life.

I was helping a close friend with a desire of his that involved an investment of money and some effort from me. In the process of helping him, we were discussing the current status and details, when to my utter astonishment he called me a liar. Saying I was stunned does not completely describe the surprise, hurt, and anger that suddenly overwhelmed me. I couldn't believe he would think or say that as I would never do this to him in this way or any other.

Try as I might, this episode affected my feelings about our relationship. We no longer got together as friends do. Our interactions were cordial, but I didn't want social time with him anymore. I knew that I needed to forgive him, but doing so was so difficult. As I pondered upon my feelings, I realized that what occurred was more than just a personal hurt. I felt truly betrayed by someone I was close to, someone that I loved.

After quite some time, I gathered myself sufficiently to exercise the courage to meet with him and discuss what had happened. In fact, it took two meetings over a period of time for me to clearly share my feelings and to completely forgive, but I did. When I had done so, an incredibly heavy burden was lifted. I felt peace and joy that had not been mine during this entire period. Being unforgiving was like poisoning the water in a well. My whole being was affected negatively by this shortcoming.

The caring I had for him returned. I was cleansed, healed, and became a new man. He told me that he didn't even remember the incident. I am now certain that he spoke only in anger at that moment and what came out was not what he really felt about me. There is an additional lesson in this, isn't there!

We load our souls with "unforgiven" burdens that are so heavy to be borne. They will not go away without our attention. They will disappear completely when we forgive. We must not forget that the "greater sin" is not to forgive. No matter what has happened to us, to follow in the Savior's footsteps we must forgive those who have hurt or sinned against us. So, forgive, no matter how hard it is. God will help us when we make the genuine effort to do so. At that time, we will be freed from a prison of our own making.

Forgiveness opportunities may become evident concerning people who are more distant from us, people that we do not even know. As I was serving in the Draper Temple one evening, I was suddenly filled with "light" and caring for someone I had never met. He was a national leadership figure and his political positions were generally uncomfortable for me. We disagreed on a number of things. In fact, I felt some sense of revulsion just hearing his voice.

I can still see where I was in the temple when my prejudice was displaced by, not a vision, but a very concerned awareness for his spiritual well-being. Suddenly, his political positions were very unimportant. All I cared about was his well-being in relationship to Truth and the Heavens.

The realization came that when we care first about the welfare of others, even someone we disagree with or dislike, the reasons for those feelings become insignificant. In this case, they went way into the background. What matters most importantly is being able to see beyond the differences between us to look upon and love them as the Savior does, to see them with eye and heart as persons of value. When we do, we may still disagree, but now we seek understanding and progression on a totally different level, one that can only be reached by the change in our hearts.

Anger

Be not hasty in thy spirit to be angry:
for anger resteth in the bosom of fools
(Ecclesiastes 7:9, emphasis added).

Wow! That seems really harsh. I've been angry in my life—no surprise, on more than one occasion. So what? Haven't you? Well, I recognize that I've done some stupid things as a result of it. I've seen holes in walls and doors, all a consequence of someone becoming angry. News reports are filled with information about physical and verbal abuse, all related to anger. Maybe this scripture is right. Maybe we are foolish to allow ourselves to get angry.

The consequences of anger may make us look silly or foolish, may hurt relationships, and can be the cause of physical destruction and personal hurt. Often these outcomes require repentance, because we commit acts that under thoughtful consideration we would not do. Anger is generally not ennobling.

It is important to recognize that there is a mortal pathway that transforms anguish into anger. It is a tough, rocky road without joy. Blaming our misfortunes on someone or something else seems to lift the burden a little at times, but it never produces peace or real happiness. When traveling this road, we can have moments of pleasure. We are inclined to pretend that this is happiness, but it is in reality a disguise designed to reduce our pain by blaming someone else. This tends to insulate us from the truth.

From a practical perspective, if what has taken place is our fault, we need to own up to it, working and praying for forgiveness. If it is truly someone else's fault, we need to forgive, that is the commandment. When in our right spiritual minds, we know the truth. The laws governing mortality have not changed, nor have we just because we are in pain. Forgiveness and the exercise of faith are the threads of divinity that need to be sewn throughout all parts of our lives. They have the power to heal and invite joy.

Unfortunately, some of us are so distraught in our pain that we fan the flames of anger and attempt to establish blame all the way to the Heavens. In finding no one else to make liable, God becomes the ultimate justification. We talk ourselves into believing that God must be responsible. This is really troubling.

There is another focus of anger that I would like to consider, one that I can empathize with. Before discussing it, I think this instruction given to Isaiah for all of us is vitally important, for God said,

> *For my thoughts are not your thoughts,*
> *neither are your ways my ways, saith the*
> *Lord. For as the heavens are higher than*
> *the earth, so are my ways higher than your*
> *ways, and my thoughts than your thoughts.*
> (Isaiah 55:8-9)

With this divine understanding, here is the question. What about those of us who become angry with God? An event happens in a person's or family's life that is out of anyone's control. With the knowledge that God is "all powerful," isn't it natural for a person to wonder why Heavenly Intervention did not come, especially if those involved felt they were doing their best with hope, prayer, and the exercise of faith? Under these conditions, could a person feel abandoned by God? I believe the answer is "yes."

These are not "corrupt" people or enemies of God. They are His children trying to make sense out of what is perceived as tragedy and the apparent lack of sought for heavenly help.

I know a family that sacrificed much in the service of God. One of their children was physically distressed, facing the possibility of death. After the exercise of faith, prayer, and Priesthood blessing, the child died. The family became confused by the interplay of anguish and hopeful, prayerful expectation. I'm sure there were painful cries of "Why did this happen?" and "Why weren't our prayers answered?" This is pain from so deep in the soul that mortal therapy may struggle to touch it. In their sorrow and anger they became inactive, angry at God to the point of trying to thrust Him from their lives.

If you have ever carried a heavy burden of despair, then you will have some idea of the challenge of this family and others like them. I'm certain that God looks upon them with great caring. There is much to learn and spiritually comprehend, especially in trusting God, that what takes place will ultimately be a blessing, even if sacrifice is required. The experience, the requirements, and the process will have redeeming value, aligning our lives much closer to Him.

The resolution, the reconciling with God, must be done in God's own way and not our own. Being angry with God will only create distance between His children and Him. This is why it is so important to understand that God's thoughts and ways are so much higher than our own, as the scriptures bear witness.

We certainly are not always aware of God's will for the people we care about and serve, or for us, individually. What we don't comprehend of God's dealings with His children, especially when accompanied by anguish can become a difficult trial. Yet, we know that trials are essential to our preparation for Eternal Life, for God's life. Hopefully, we have not forgotten that God loves us, whether saint or sinner. We need to remember that the complete plan for mortal life was prepared by Him. There are no surprises. What is done here is done with His foreknowledge.

These two scriptures shine a bright light on the reality of trials or "chastening" as one scripture describes it and "why" they occur.

> *Wherein ye greatly rejoice, though now for a season, if need be, ye are in heaviness through manifold temptations:*

> *That the trial of your faith, being much more precious than of gold that perisheth, though it be tried with fire, might be found unto praise and honour and glory*

at the appearing of Jesus Christ
(1 Peter 1:6-7).

And ye have forgotten the exhortation
which speaketh unto you as unto children,
My son, despise not thou the chastening of
the Lord, nor faint when thou art rebuked
of him:

For whom the Lord loveth he chasteneth,
and scourgeth every son whom he receiveth.

If ye endure chastening, God dealeth
with you as with sons; for what son is he
whom the father chasteneth not
(Hebrews 12:5-7)?

Though the language in these scriptures may be different than how we might express it, the message should be very clear. We don't know God's will; we will be tried, and it will always turn to our blessing if we accept it in faith. This language is so beautiful. The trial of our faith, "though it be tried with fire, might be found unto praise and honour and glory at the appearing of Jesus Christ." This scripture fills me with such hope for the future and the Heavens desired outcome of our lives.

I hope you know what it feels like to be under the profound influence of the Spirit, to feel the exhilaration, the peace, the joy, even joy in sorrowing as light fills both heart and mind. Even the quiet whisperings of the Spirit are filled with peace and a sense and recognition of "right" and light. I bear witness that nurturing from the Spirit is a gift available to all of God's children, to each of us without discrimination. We just need to be willing to receive it.

My wife and I lost a daughter to congenital heart disease when she was 20 years old. I believe I can appreciate the challenge of dealing with deep personal tragedy. I have found though that God does not leave us alone to face it. At her passing, the Spirit wrapped us in a cloak of remarkable Heavenly Love. We knew God has been and continues to be in charge. We sorrowed at her passing. No day goes by without feeling her absence, but we are also filled with confirmed knowledge that this fits into God's plan.

This statement of the Savior's is the balm that can heal any heavy heart:

> *Come unto me, all ye that labour and*
> *are heavy laden, and I will give you rest.*
> *Take my yoke upon you, and learn of me;*
> *for I am meek and lowly in heart: and ye*
> *shall find rest unto your souls. For my yoke*
> *is easy, and my burden is light* (Matthew
> 11:28-30).

The Savior is doing the work the Father gave Him to do. Christ has made it "perfectly" clear that our Father in Heaven is perfect, so is Jesus Christ. Therefore, Father and Son deal perfectly with Father's children. There can be no exceptions or neither one would be a God.

It is important that we do not lose sight and connection with the instruction to "Take my yoke upon you, and learn of me." To take His yoke upon us is to partner with Him in the work of salvation for all of Father's children. He says that He is "meek and lowly in heart," the very qualities we should be praying and striving for in order to "partner with Him." He is the perfect example and partner!

Alma, giving guidance to an apostate Nephite lawyer in Ammonihah, made this statement in reference to the Judgment:

> *. . . we must come forth and stand before*
> *him in his glory, and in his power, and*
> *in his might, majesty, and dominion, and*
> *acknowledge to our everlasting shame that*
> *all his judgments are just; that he is just in*
> *all his works, and that he is merciful unto*
> *the children of men, and that he has all*
> *power to save every man that believeth on*
> *his name and bringeth forth fruit meet for*
> *repentance.* (Alma 12:15)

Father does not deal unfairly with His children, that is my testimony. We cannot see us as He sees us, knows us, and has plans for us. This perfect Parent asks us to align our lives with His will. There is nothing to be gained trying to get God to align His flawless will with our imperfect one. In mortal or eternal logic, that makes no sense.

If some of us have spent years and great amounts of energy building a wall around ourselves in anger at God, do we expect an apology, when in reality He has done nothing, but what is in our best interest? Being far from perfect, we must be cautious. If in building our wall of separation, having worked long and hard to maintain it, we must not let pride keep us from admitting that we are wrong.

I know pride personally and I know how hard it is to give it up. God's mercy has been so evident in the "Heavenly Orchestration" of my life's experiences. Pride must not take the place of truth and light. Anger or temper tantrums have no value. Turning from anger and pride is ennobling and within the Divine Will. We will receive mercy and forgiveness as we turn our challenges over to the Savior.

Being Comfortable

For behold, thus saith the Lord God: I will give unto the children of men line upon line, precept upon precept, here a little and there a little; and blessed are those who hearken unto my precepts, and lend an ear unto my counsel, for they shall learn wisdom; for unto him that receiveth I will give more; and from them that shall say, We have enough, from them shall be taken away even that which they have (2 Nephi 28:30, emphasis added).

God intends for us to continue learning throughout our entire mortal sojourn, as evidenced by this scripture. Our ability to learn changes as time and varying experiences prepare us for what will yet come. Often as adults, we don't see ourselves as children, needing the care and instruction of a Parent. Yet, when one honestly ponders what mortality is all about and how it fits into God's plan for His children, it becomes clear that we must trust our Parent to teach us what is needed for our successful progression in becoming a complete Adult, as He is.

You may not remember the coaching, coaxing, and physical encouragement needed to teach you how to walk, but it was there. As you got older, your observation and memory abilities improved. You gained the capacity to begin to comprehend cause and effect. You made mistakes, like touching a hot stove, but learned not to do it again. Those of us who are a little more "hardheaded" had to prove that outcome a few more times before changing our behavior, but experience taught us how to improve and manage our lives.

Do you remember your youthful determination to be independent? I'm sure you constantly tried to prove that you were equal to the tasks and challenges of growing up. "Mommy, I can do it myself."

Hopefully, you had caring family and friends to mentor and show you how this temporal world works. Gaining creature comforts became a natural part of your daily effort and existence. That effort did not change as you grew older, it just changed in complexity.

Teenagers become adults, parents, and responsible parties for temporal living. Varying talents, abilities, and circumstances provide different opportunities for worldly possessions and gains. Some have more, some less. Temporal life doesn't seem to be built to make us all equal in abilities and possessions. So, there must be another purpose.

Being social creatures, we often measure ourselves against others and may be motivated to try to duplicate what others have and seem to enjoy. Those worldly desires can easily become a priority for attainment over other more worthwhile endeavors. After all, we have been trying to prove "we can do it" most all of our lives.

I originally went to school with the desire for a career in medicine, far different from the one I ended up with. A different or altered path appeared following college graduation. I decided on business, ultimately ending up self-employed.

At an early stage of this career, I thought that maybe I should go back to school for an MBA. My business partner and I were working with a business school professor from one of the universities in our state. I expressed my interest in an advanced degree and he talked me out of it, saying that I would be bored, after making my way in the real world.

I didn't go back to school and in retrospect, I wonder about the decision. Was it good? Was it bad? Years ago, I had many opportunities to wish I had done things differently. Not always knowing what is best for me, I had to trust that the "no" decision set me up for some experiences I really needed and may not have had with a different situation. I feel I recognize Godly purpose a little better now, years later. I know that understanding will continue to develop with clarity improving over time and with experience. I no longer feel I made a bad decision, but the decision I needed for my development as a son of God, a husband and a father.

We had periods of financial sufficiency and others of scraping by when I was out of work. My sweetheart went back to teaching school when our youngest child was old enough for elementary school. It was her efforts as a special education teacher that kept us going. My business career bounced around through several industries with me finally ending up as a business skills trainer.

When the economic collapse occurred in 2008, I lost my job. For the next seven years, I tried to find work in the areas in which I had some experience, but without success. I had some short-term opportunities, but after a while these disappeared as well. Without an advanced degree I really wasn't an expert in anything in the eyes of the world.

At long last, I came to the point when I had to do something. I probably should have made that decision earlier, but I had been hanging on to the hope and desire to do what I enjoy, what I feel I am good at. I finally determined to go and get any job I could, discarding the idea of finding work in an area and at a "level" that interested me. You need to know that this desperation was so humbling that I began looking for entry-level work in an area that was uncomfortable for me and with companies that I had no prior interest in, but they were hiring.

I found a job with a company that was literally at the top of my "I don't want to list." It is important to know of the deep gratitude that fills my soul that circumstances conspired to encourage me to become an employee of this company, Walmart. (This may be one of the most important turning points in my life.) Swallowing my pride was difficult and distasteful, kind of like swallowing . . . well, anything that turns your taste buds against you.

Opportunities continued to come and I was there only a few weeks, but it was a blessing, a tender mercy. I hope this is clear with this new job we were getting by, meaning we were making all the important payments, but our meager savings was disappearing and credit card debt wasn't. I certainly didn't see us as living in luxury, especially living paycheck to paycheck.

In a rare pause at work, the Spirit spoke clearly to my mind and heart, *"What is more important to you, experience or being comfortable?"* I was stunned! I knew the source and felt a sense of awe that the Lord, through the Spirit, would take notice of me at this time and place. I didn't feel comfortable, yet here was a spiritual prompting designed to get me to ponder and make a decision regarding an important focus of life investment.

My thought processing was not immobilized, so I immediately focused on what I assumed should be the correct answer, "experience of course." But, in being honest, I knew that this answer may not correctly identify my true feelings. I was mentally and emotionally churning. Thoughts flew in and out of my mind like confetti in the wind as various emotions stirred the recesses of my soul. This question caused me to look deep within.

Customers lined up once again and I was reluctantly transported back to the work at hand, the shadow of the Inquiry never left my mind.

Many months have separated the present from this experience, but "the question" had been successfully planted in my heart, to be reviewed often. It has become a standard against which I do some periodic evaluating. I now know where I stand and can answer the question honestly.

All of this begs this question, is there a difference between comfort and being comfortable? If so, what is it? We were blessed with the comfort that comes from having the necessities of life and, if honest, many luxuries not enjoyed throughout the world. Then, what did the Spirit mean by "being comfortable?" Isn't it all right to be comfortable?

Understanding for me came. I'm certain that it was quietly orchestrated by the Spirit. I began to comprehend that "being comfortable" isn't necessarily about all of our creature comforts, but it is all about our priorities and goals.

A key component of my emotional chaos was trying to match the lifestyle of the people around us. Even though I tried not to be envious, I was. We had what we needed temporally, but at times I felt underprivileged as we saw what our friends could do and enjoy. I tried to put on a "satisfied" face and demeanor, but I wasn't settled.

This Heaven directed life review seemed designed to get me to declare what I would make most important in my life, the pursuit of the temporal (being comfortable) or experiences that will make of me a better man, a man of God. Would I trust God to get me where I need to be and to be doing what He would have me do? Would I be loyal to Him?

Be honest. What are you working for in this life? How does this relate to the reason for your existence? I recall from the description of Adam and Eve's journey that

> In the sweat of thy face shalt thou eat
> bread, till thou return unto the ground . .
> . (Genesis 3:19).

That sounds like "comfort" is not the focus and purpose of life, but "experience" is. Our first parents must have been comfortable in the Garden of Eden, but staying there would not have allowed them to complete their life's mission. Being cast out provided the experience needed for them to be "elevated" and worthy to return home to Father.

I don't even question now that I needed a change of priorities, even though on the employment scale I was on the bottom rung, just up from unemployed. That is not where I am now. Pondering upon the kinds of experiences needed in life is an interesting mental and spiritual exercise. Where in life's guidebook is the page devoted to me and my needs? What support should I search for or embrace if something unrequested or uncomfortable is at my doorstep?

The first guideline that comes to mind is God's declaration that His work and His glory is

> . . . to bring to pass the immortality and
> eternal life of man (Moses 1:39).

This is His work and because I am His child, is it my work? The scriptures seem very clear, that it is.

Two other "searching instructions" quickly come to mind. The first is from the 13th Article of Faith (13 brief statements of gospel belief and application written by Joseph Smith for the Church of Jesus Christ of Latter-Day Saints):

> *If there is anything virtuous, lovely, or of good report or praiseworthy, we seek after these things.*

This statement does not need a great deal of explanation. It summarizes what God's children ought to be looking for as they make decisions about every aspect of living.

The second guidance is given from President Gordon B. Hinkley, the prophet and president of The Church of Jesus Christ of Latter-Day Saints at the time of this writing. He has encouraged all of us to get all the education we can. We are able to take education and experience with us when we depart mortality. Remember this instruction from 2 Nephi 28:30 about the Lord's promise?

> *. . . for unto him that receiveth I will give more.*

Doesn't it excite you to consider receiving all the education you can regarding God's work and our lives here?

Another scripture from latter-day revelation seems important.

> *Whatever principle of intelligence we attain unto in this life, it will rise with us in the resurrection. And if a person gains more knowledge and intelligence in this life through his diligence and obedience than another, he will have so much the advantage in the world to come* (D&C 130:18-19).

Obtaining intelligence or education is not a race. God has made it very clear that He wants to give us, every child, all the education we are willing to receive. That education will come within varied life experiences. Those who are willing to receive and invest themselves throughout their lives will obviously have progressed further in receiving all that God has for His children, even Eternal Life.

On the "dark" side of this, remember that God has instructed in 2 Nephi 28:30 that if a person says, "I have enough," the consequence is to have taken from him "that which he has already received." God's "plan of happiness" or salvation has one intended outcome, for us to be worthy and prepared to return Home. This requires us to desire education and experience all of our lives. It will come in many forms, but embracing it thankfully is so important.

Remember,

> *Thou shalt thank the Lord thy God in*
> *all things* (D&C 59:7).

What motivates you? What are you seeking for? Are you striving to enlarge your soul by embracing new experiences or is "being comfortable" your priority? By turning to the world, making its gifts, its comforts your priority, you face a real outcome of the numbing of your spirit to Heavenly interventions and inspiration.

Either we are willing to embrace new experiences or we are effectively telling the Lord, "We have enough," thus setting ourselves up to have what we have spiritually gained taken away. In the language of the scriptures, we may very well be damning (I like this word in this context) ourselves, because our progression ceases. This is the connection between my experience and the instruction from 2 Nephi 28:30.

So, what is most important to you? Mortal life is designed to provide either option. You choose.

Let me bring you up to date. My employment challenge was answered over time and with steps in a process that has blessed me beyond earthly value. I was invited to accept my last career move as an academic advisor for Salt Lake Community College. I loved the work, the service, and could never have been prepared without the challenging experiences referred to earlier.

Gateway to Eternal Life

Why are so many willing to give so much in order to receive the blessings of the temple? Those who understand the eternal blessings which come from the temple ordinances, such as marriage, know that no sacrifice is too great, no price too heavy, no struggle too difficult in order to receive those blessings. There are never too many miles to travel, too many obstacles to overcome, or too much discomfort to endure. They understand that the saving ordinances received in the temple permit us to someday return to our Heavenly Father in an eternal family relationship. We will be endowed with blessings and power from on high as we make progress on this sacred path of life, which is worth every sacrifice and effort.

"Until you have entered this house of the Lord and received all the blessings which await you there, you have not obtained everything the Church has to offer. The all-important and crowning blessings of membership in the Church are those blessings which we receive in the temples of God"
(The Holy Temple—a Beacon to

the World, April 2011 General Conference, Thomas S. Monson).

I have lived long enough and, due to the grace of God, have experienced enough to know that this instruction from a prophet of God is true. The Spirit has confirmed this with a collaboration of feelings I cannot describe, but the outcome has brought both peace and passion to my being. I can say in all honesty, I have been given "light" to see. This tender mercy extends beyond my poor temporal comprehension. I can see and feel. Conversion burns within me. I don't know how to say it any differently. I hope I have a striving disciple's perception.

Looking backwards in time, it is interesting to examine where I started and where I am now. The first time I went to the temple to receive the sacred saving ordinances performed there was in preparation to serve a full-time proselyting mission for the Church. I received my endowment of blessings in the Salt Lake Temple. My parents escorted me and my dad guided me through the ordinance.

My summary of the experience is probably best described in this way, "What did I just do? Is this really the church I know?" The symbolism and ritual were so foreign to me that I was very uncomfortable. I believe I went twice before leaving for the New England Mission. Those two times didn't seem to help my understanding or comfort level very much, but this is not the end of the story.

This first temple experience may have been one of the factors that caused me to call and make an appointment, while in the mission home preparing for my departure, to visit with Elder Thomas S. Monson, who was in the Quorum of the Twelve Apostles at that time. I was very uncomfortable with what was taking place, because it was so foreign to the worship I was used to in our chapels and homes. However, I was anxious about doing the right thing.

My testimony, which appeared to me to have begun fraying a bit around the edges due to the pressure I felt, was enough to get me to his office. My father knew him in high school and that is why I called him. He graciously visited with me and calmed my fears. I knew at that point that he was an apostle. That spiritual confirmation was very clear.

Following my mission, I went back to attending the temple. I felt more resolve to come to understand the ceremony and ordinances. Even though I was not drawn to ritual and all the symbolism, I came to know that the way Home was through the temple portal.

At different periods, I was able to attend the temple weekly. I came to understand President Ezra Taft Benson's (former Church president) comment that he always came out of the temple stronger than when he went in. Paying attention to my temple experiences, I realized that was the natural blessing I also received.

As the years progressed, the desire to be both a patron and an ordinance worker in the temple filled me. I asked my bishop to submit my name for consideration. A couple of months later, the invitation came to serve in the Draper Temple. I call it an invitation, because working in the temple is a voluntary "call" or opportunity.

The Draper Temple is dear to my wife and me, because we had been asked to be guides during the open house before its dedication and to be receptionists in one of the ordinance rooms. This sacred house became "our house."

My service was thankfully given for seven years as an ordinance worker, even though I have been a patron for over 50 years. All of those years and the attendant experiences changed me, even elevated my thinking. Temple thoughts were pervasive throughout the week, always peaking at the time of service. Cleansing, healing, and conversion took place within my soul. I witnessed God blessing His children in ways that were sacred, remarkable, and often so very personal.

Godly inspiration is given to temple workers to carry out Heavenly instruction. God authorizes and inspires the work done in the temples and provides all that is necessary for the ordinances to be performed properly unto completion. The Spirit provides light and understanding beyond mortal comprehension. These sacred houses are His Houses and He oversees all that takes place within them.

As a patron, I recently went to the temple with two ancestor names, one of my wife's and one of mine, to have the proxy baptisms and confirmations completed. I watched as a sister was baptized for my wife's dead relative. Suddenly, I was so overcome as to be unable to speak and I began to weep. The realization came that this sister's wait, which was on the other side of the veil that separates our mortal world from the spiritual, for this ordinance to be performed for her was over and that it was received by her with great longing and thanksgiving.

When the time came for the confirmations, being an ordained holder the of the Priesthood, I was invited to perform them. Once again, I was so overcome that I began to weep. My throat was so constricted that I was nearly unable to speak the words of the ordinance. The witness that these ordinances were received with great joy was profoundly evident, providing confirmation once again as to the reality and necessity of this Heavenly work.

Temples are the sacred gathering places for God's family, for our families, and the doors through which we must pass to go Home and live with Him.

Experiences Needed to Know Christ

For behold, the Spirit of Christ is given to every man, that he may know good from evil; wherefore, I show unto you the way to judge; for every thing which inviteth to do good, and to persuade to believe in Christ, is sent forth by the power and gift of Christ; wherefore ye may know with a perfect knowledge it is of God.

But whatsoever thing persuadeth men to do evil, and believe not in Christ, and deny him, and serve not God, then ye may know with a perfect knowledge it is of the devil; for after this manner doth the devil work, for he persuadeth no man to do good, no, not one; neither do his angels; neither do they who subject themselves unto him (**Moroni 7:16-17, emphasis added**).

Think about the experiences you have had in your life. I'm certain that you have found, as I have, that there is a difference between those that influenced you to draw nearer to God and those that have encouraged greater separation. Discernible difference exists between that which is good and that which is not.

Moroni recorded this instruction from the Lord in the Book of Ether, which is in the Book of Mormon.

And whatsoever thing persuadeth men to do good is of me; for good cometh of none save it be of me. I am the same that leadeth men to all good; . . . I am the light, and the life, and the truth of the world (Ether 4:12).

The Lord instructs in D&C 84:44,

For you shall live by every word that proceedeth forth from the mouth of God.

The Father and Son embody all that is good and true. Their word is exactly that. Verse 45 in that same section says,

For the word of the Lord is truth, and whatsoever is truth is light, and whatsoever is light is Spirit, even the Spirit of Jesus Christ.

Truth, light, Spirit, goodness, all exist within and are fundamental to the spiritual framework of our existence. We have been given the Light of Christ so that we can recognize the Spirit in all of its expressions. What a loving gift this is!

It is obvious that Light and darkness are vastly different. They look and feel different to our spirits. That which is "good" is constructive. That which is not is destructive. Spiritual darkness has no Light, truth, or goodness, having no component that is a part of our spiritual makeup. It is devoid of everything that is ennobling. It is an enemy to Light and God.

Who is the author and source of spiritual darkness? He who we call the devil and all those who have established allegiance with him. Be aware! The adversary is capable of producing imitations of good, or attempting to use the aura of good in an evil way, so we must be cautious. Those efforts are designed to be seductive, to confuse, and to divert us from embracing light and truth and will never invite or persuade to believe in Jesus Christ. This is fundamental in looking for experiences that are constructive and will prepare us to receive more and more Light.

God has made it very clear that we can come to know good from evil with a perfect knowledge, because we have each been given the Light of Christ. If a person or an experience seems to be focused on persuading us to

> *. . . do evil, and believe not in Christ,*
> *and deny him, and serve not God, then ye*
> *may know with a perfect knowledge it is of*
> *the devil* (Moroni 7:17).

Our responsibility is to learn and identify what is truly good and what is not. That which we embrace will either support and strengthen our souls or damage them.

It is true that we have been sent to the earth without memory of our life before mortality. This fact places each of us on a quest to find and embrace truth, discovering that we have not been left alone or desolate in any way in that search. Father has provided the means to complete this quest in a way that prompts or inspires the growth and progression needed to return to His Home.

From our first day of mortal life, we have received the gift of the Light of Christ to direct our thoughts and actions toward truth and corresponding light (D&C 84:46-47). This is no trivial gift as I have already said. When embraced and permitted to influence our thoughts and actions, it will lead us to reception of inspiration from the Holy Ghost and then, following baptism, to receive the Gift of the Holy Ghost and the opportunity of His companionship. These spiritual bestowals will guide us to the source of all truth and Light, Jesus Christ, the Savior. We have been charged to learn to use these gifts and trust God to guide us throughout mortality to become true disciples of Christ.

With this information as a foundation, what must we do to come to know the Savior? What experiences are necessary? It is no surprise that we need desire. It doesn't matter how that desire is generated, even if it is by the mistakes we have made. With desire and repentance, a destructive pathway can be redirected to righteousness.

Some of God's children have had remarkable experiences with angels, even with the Savior himself. Consider those people that were visited by the Savior in the new world, following His resurrection. Wouldn't you consider it an incredible blessing? I would. Yet the Savior gave this instruction:

> . . . *Blessed are ye if ye shall give heed unto the words of these twelve whom I have chosen from among you to minister unto you, and to be your servants . . . therefore blessed are ye if ye shall believe in me and be baptized, after that ye have seen me and know that I am.*
>
> *And again, more blessed are they who shall believe in your words because that ye shall testify that ye have seen me, and that ye know that I am. Yea, blessed are they who shall believe in your words, and come down into the depths of humility and be baptized, for they shall be visited with fire and with the Holy Ghost, and shall receive a remission of their sins* (3 Nephi 12:1-2).

"More blessed" would be those who heard and believed the testimonies of the witnesses of Jesus's arrival and teachings. That is a very striking pronouncement and clearly indicates to me that I don't need to see the Savior to have a testimony of Jesus Christ. I just need to have the "good" experiences that are possible for me to choose. If I do, then I will receive or be "visited with fire and the Holy Ghost." I need nothing more than to continue choosing that which is "good."

Experiences Transforming My Life

In every life there are those milestones that are transformative, such as baptism, receiving one's endowment, and marriage in God's temple. I want to share with you some experiences that have changed how I think, feel, and who I am. These are not the regular milestones of life. I see in them the Hand of the Lord providing experiences and education that may be unique in their impact on me and are vital to my progression. God does not perform inconsequential works. I have come to know them as ennobling and will share them in random order.

Early in my marriage, I was emotionally upside-down regarding employment. I felt I had three options, one of which was to just stay where I was. By the way, this option was totally unacceptable to me, at least emotionally. Needing to make a decision, anxious about the present and future, I decided to fast and pray until I got an answer. If the fast went beyond one day, I was determined to see it through to the end.

Dinnertime of day one passed and I moved on to day two. Around 9:00 p.m., (This experience had such a profound effect upon me, that I remember much of the details, even after many years.) I decided to go into my bedroom and offer prayer as I had several times earlier in the day.

I began, as I had each of those times, by rehearsing the options as I saw them, but I only remember one now, "keeping things as they are." I pondered upon them as I rehearsed them and a powerful thought interrupted my prayerful inquiry, "What if the Lord instructs me to continue what I have been doing? No change. Can I do it? Will I do it?"

The idea of no change taking place was so distasteful to me that I had not even considered that this option might be directed by the Lord. I was so stunned by that thought that I ended my prayer and stayed on my knees. I realized that the Spirit had spoken to me. I was deeply concerned about my ability to accept the Lord's will, if it wasn't what I hoped for. What if He told me to do what I didn't want to do? Could I change and do it?

As I pondered on this, I realized that if I wasn't going to do what the Lord asked, if I wasn't willing to do whatever He asked, what is the value of asking for His help at all? What I was doing was counselling Him on how to answer me. I knew that He would not instruct me to do anything I was unwilling to do. That being the case, without a change of mind, I discerned I would not receive any counsel at all.

I stayed on my knees and wrestled with my thoughts and emotions, now that I knew what was required of me in principle. Finally, I came to the level of commitment that I would do whatever I was instructed, even if it wasn't the answer I wanted.

I opened my prayer as before and the answer came immediately. I wasn't surprised and knew that I was to continue on as I had been. Perhaps you can appreciate the conflict of pleasure in receiving personal revelation and of discomfort from committing to doing that which was painful for me.

Life went on as the Lord intended and I, through this ennobling experience, gained a greater understanding of God and His love for us, as we strive to follow the path He desires. I learned something of commitment and conversion.

Later on in my business career, my partner and I were acting as investment advisers for small pension plans, mostly medical professionals. A significant portion of our work was in real estate. A commercial real estate developer approached us to see if our clients would make a loan on raw ground that he wanted to develop. After reviewing the details, we thought this would be a good investment and agreed to put the loan together.

As you have probably experienced in buying, selling, or obtaining a real estate loan, someone needs to serve as an escrow agent. This individual handles putting together all "closing" parts of the transaction, including the signing of documents and disbursal of any funds involved. The developer had a person he wanted to serve as the escrow agent and after legal review, we agreed to his request.

Our attorney researched all the legalities, put the documents together, and got everything ready for the closing. The day the loan was to be made, I woke up feeling very uncomfortable about the transaction. I called our attorney, explained how I felt and asked him how he felt about the transaction and all of the details. He told me he didn't see any problems. His response put a small emotional Band-Aid on my feelings. They didn't go away, but we went ahead and closed the loan anyway.

The next morning, I got a call from our attorney. He had just heard on the news that the escrow agent had been arrested for fraud. You can imagine how I felt, depression and fear deeper and darker than I had ever experienced filled me. Hundreds of thousands of our clients' dollars were at stake. I can't begin to describe the pain, anger, and horror that filled my mind and body. I have experienced panic before, but this was on a whole new level. This malady would not go away very quickly.

We found out soon enough that our clients' money was gone, really gone, having been used by this agent to cover his other misdeeds. After years of legal wrangling, we never recovered one penny that had been lost.

That was a tough experience, that went on for years. As with most of life's difficult experiences, by being obedient and exercising faith, the negative turned to positive. Throughout it all I felt the Lord's supportive hand. The misjudgment was mine, but there was transformative power in the journey.

There are a number of lessons that could be learned from this tragedy, but the one that quickly became the most important to me was the realization that the "negative" feeling I had was a prompting of the Holy Ghost. I didn't recognize what it was and in following up, I turned to the wisdom of man instead of the wisdom of God. You can see how well that turned out.

We did our best to try to make everything as right as we could for our clients, given so little to work with. They could have made life very difficult, but kindness ruled the day.

I made the Lord a promise that from that time on I would always obey every spiritual prompt. This meant that I needed to learn to recognize them. I can say that from this time forward I have strived with far greater intensity and determination to recognize Heavenly whispering and to obey.

Can this failure be an ennobling experience? Absolutely, if it precipitated changes within me. My ability to recognize the Spirit and my determination to be obedient began a progression that I shall always be grateful for. This tragedy has fueled an ennobling change in who I am and how I now attempt to live my life, to align it with God's will.

Our oldest child was a daughter born with congenital heart disease. That came as a surprise as we have no history on either side of the family. In fact, we have two children with this malady. As you can appreciate, we started early in family life to have experiences not expected in our lifetime.

Children with our daughter's problem had lived into their teens at this time. That was all the hope and expectation medical science could give us. She had heart surgery at day two and lived until she was 20. She was blessed beyond mortal expectation.

Our daughter had multiple problems beyond heart disease and at the time of her death, needed both a heart and lung transplant, which she was not a candidate for. She was in and out of medical institutions so often, that even as a baby she associated the color white as a medical color, a doctor's uniform. In my job, I had to wear white shirts. We learned quickly that if I wanted to hold her when I got home from work, I had to change shirts. If I didn't, she would cry immediately when I picked her up. Putting on a colored shirt produced the warm welcome I had hoped to receive.

I don't know how many times she was in the hospital for varying treatments and life-threatening issues throughout her life, but I wager that it was in the neighborhood of 80-100. We knew most of the caregivers at Primary Children's Medical Center in the cardiac unit.

Our experiences ranged from the traumatic to the sublime. Everyone in our family came to understand the relationship she had with the Heavens. It seemed remarkable to those of us who had not yet progressed as far as she had on the path to the Tree of Life (1 Nephi 8:10-34), to Christ and His love. She was a gift to all of us.

I will never forget her last few days with us. She was back in the Medical Center on Tuesday. The doctors said that if she improved, she could go home on Friday. When one of our friends asked her about going home, she told her she was going home on Thursday. I attempted to correct her, but she seemed not to notice.

On Thursday, her condition rapidly deteriorated. That afternoon she went Home, just as she said she would. We discovered then that she knew when her mortal transfer would take place and she would be sent to her Heavenly Home.

The twenty years of following in her spiritual footsteps was a remarkable experience for me—spiritually-life changing. Every day of her entire life, but especially that last day, opened my soul to spiritual understanding that I wondered if I could have received in any other way. The effect was so profound that I wrote a book about it and the blessing of her life within mine. It was written with my family readership in mind, *Turtletoes, Following the Steps of An Angel*.

The experiences that refine and advance us on the path of Eternal Life of being worthy to return to our Father's Home are frequently challenging, difficult, and sometimes painful. They have intrinsic rewards that are glorious beyond comprehension and description, both here and in the hereafter. I have had a therapeutic glimpse.

I have witnessed beauty in so many different ways and have been filled with a profound sense of thanksgiving and awe. Eyes, ears, touch, taste, and smell have all provided input, but the result is so much grander than even the sum of the parts.

It has become so obvious to me that mortality introduces and facilitates changes in our souls that are beyond our comprehension and dreams. I can feel them and yet I cannot describe them. They give me a sense of being that seems to lift me beyond the rigors of mortal life at times. Perhaps these changes are contributors and components of being worthy to receive Eternal Life, God's life. That wouldn't surprise me.

Have you ever looked at something as simple as a leaf beyond its place on the plant? The shape, color, texture, and venation seem to be visual poetry. A leaf is an organ with pores for the input and output of gases and specialized for photosynthesis. It looks to be so simple "on the surface" yet is so complex, bearing witness of a Creator.

"Mother Earth" loves to give gifts. Consider an orange tree and the feast it produces for all of our mortal senses. How beautiful for the eye it is with its shape and colors, especially when adorned with the flowers that will become the fruit. Have you smelled the blossoms? Absolutely intoxicating.

When you've taken the fruit in hand, have you enjoyed the feel of its smooth skin, but with patterned depressions that delight the sense of touch. Upon removing the peel, the change in the atmosphere is almost magical and the aroma tickles and delights our sense of smell. Finally, the sensation of taste and smell combine to feed our body and lift our spirits.

Consider the experience of sitting outside, listening to falling rain and imbibing the incredible fragrance, so clean, so unique, so refreshing, and healing. Have you ever stood on the edge of a lake, all alone, and skipped a stone across it, watching the ripples spreading and converging while the tranquility of the experience infused new life into your being? Or, have you sat at the beach, watching and listening to breaking waves, "eye and ear candy," a gift sent by God to calm a troubled heart and lift the spirit.

How boring and incomplete would be our world without sunrises and sunsets, lakes, mountains, deserts and animals of all description. Beauty for all of the senses and the soul is everywhere, if we pay attention and choose to embrace experiences that provide appreciation and enjoyment. Turn off your technology. Experience the world around you utilizing the spirit of the Giver. Everything that is here has been bestowed upon us by a Loving Father and our Lord Jesus Christ for our blessing and delight.

Becoming One

---

*And the Father and I are one. I am
in the Father and the Father in me;
and inasmuch as ye have received me,
ye are in me and I in you*
(D&C 50:43, emphasis added).

*Neither pray I for these alone, but
for them also which shall believe on
me through their word; That they all
may be one; as thou, Father, art in me,
and I in thee, that they also may be
one in us; that the world may believe
that thou hast sent me*
(John 17:20-21, emphasis added).

These two scriptures bear a powerful witness that we not only can become one with the Savior and the Father, but that it is their desire that we do so. Mortality is designed for that Heavenly Family goal to be achieved, one child at a time, through experience and each child's responses to it.

Oneness isn't reflective of the incomprehensible description conceived by some regarding Father, Son, and Holy Ghost. It is accomplished on the spirit level, when we each align our hearts, thoughts, and actions with the will of Father.

This scripture in John is from the Savior's Intercessory Prayer. Read the entire prayer. Its spirit and message will take you beyond the clouds to draw you nearer to the Heavens.

It appears that there are two competing options for oneness, being one with the "world" or one with Jehovah and Elohim, with Son and Father. In my mind, the Godly revealed sacramental prayers clearly and simply state that Heavenly Oneness can begin to be ours in this life.

When we partake of the sacrament, we are participating in an ordinance that requires certain vital covenants, (1) that we are willing to take upon us the Savior's name, (2) that we will always remember Him, and (3) that we will keep His commandments. If we do so, we are promised that we will have His Spirit to be with us. (D&C 20:77, 79)

Can you see in the sacramental ordinance the principle of Oneness? We take upon us His name, remember Him, and keep His commandments. In addition, we consume bread and water as if it were His flesh and blood, making us one with Him, and we are promised that we will have His spirit to be with us.

As can be seen from these two scriptures and this sacred ordinance, through "spirit" interrelationship we can become one with the Savior and Father.

I'm certain that Oneness takes place through "baby steps" in mortality. The feeling I have when I've done something right and the Spirit confirms it; the result is so incredibly sweet and fulfilling. I can only imagine what it must feel like to be totally One. I'll keep taking baby steps and cherishing life's ennobling experiences as they come. Focus and energy spent will be the determinants.

Joy

Adam fell that men might be; and
men are, that they might have joy
(2 Nephi 2:25, emphasis added).

This doctrine is simple. Where we mortals create personal chaos is in the choices we make. The "fall of Adam and Eve in the Garden of Eden" came about so that all of Father's children could come to the earth and that in becoming mortal and progressing, they "might have joy." This instruction to the prophet Joseph Smith explains much about the need for mortality.

> _For man is spirit. The elements_
> _are eternal, and spirit and element,_
> _inseparably connected receive a fulness_
> _of joy; And when separated, man cannot_
> _receive a fulness of joy_ (D&C 93:33-34).

A fullness of joy is not possible when spirit and body are separated. This explains another reason for the resurrection, so that we can have joy eternally.

These scriptures lead me to wonder what joy is, where does it come from and have I ever really experienced it. Here are several scriptures, both ancient and modern, that answer these questions.

The Apostle Paul in his instructions to the Galatians delineated the negative works of the flesh, such as envying and hatred, all of which will keep those who do them out of the "kingdom of God." He then says,

> _The fruit of the Spirit is love, joy, peace,_
> _longsuffering, gentleness, goodness, faith,_

meekness, temperance: . . .
(Galatians 5:22-23).

The association of joy with these righteous characteristics is unmistakable and suggests that joy is a gift, a "fruit" of the Spirit.

Joseph Smith received this instruction from the Lord about reception of the Spirit.

> *Verily, verily, I say unto you, I will impart unto you of my Spirit, which shall enlighten your mind, which shall fill your soul with joy* (D&C 11:13).

By receiving the Spirit, Joseph's mind would be enlightened or instruction in truth given and the Spirit would fill his soul with joy. This gift is for all of Father's children when we receive the Spirit and hold on to the gifts given.

Consider this instruction from the Lord to Joseph on the Sabbath day.

> *And on this day thou shalt do none other thing, only let thy food be prepared with singleness of heart that thy fasting* (hungering and thirsting after righteousness) *may be perfect, or in other words, that thy joy may be full* (D&C 59:13, emphasis added).

From here, we learn that hungering and thirsting after righteousness invites a fullness of joy. Since joy is a gift or fruit of the Spirit, this makes perfect sense and provides the answer for how joy is obtained.

> *If ye keep my commandments, ye shall abide in my love; even as I have kept my Father's commandments, and abide in his love. These things have I spoken unto you, that my joy might remain in you, and that your joy might be full* (John 15:10-11).

This beautiful instruction through the Apostle John makes it clear that to have a fullness of joy and for it to continue, we must keep the Savior's commandments to "abide" in His love. This is exactly the relationship Jesus has with His Father.

Our mortal world offers many opportunities for pleasure, fun, and happiness. Other variations of this theme might include: contentment, satisfaction, cheerfulness, merriment, gaiety, joviality, glee, bliss, and delight. We might even call it "joy."

In trying to understand what joy feels like, what it is at least to my mortal senses, I went back to a time of great happiness in our family. My wife and I decided to buy a boat. The women in my life, mother, wife, and daughter all let me know together that it was time. In my effort at being obedient, we found one to our liking. We decided to give it to the family for Christmas. You can probably appreciate the fun we had with the plans and anticipation of our children finding it Christmas morning.

We were not disappointed. That is one of the happiest times in my life. I look back on it with such thanksgiving. In this temporal realm joy appears to affect our souls in a much deeper way than that which is fun or pleasurable. I classify our boat experience as joy because it impacted our family members together, something that is a significant part of who we are. In my mind and heart, it approaches the spiritual in its content and family impact. Joy has also filled my soul with personal achievement and growth. There are so many ways we can experience it here.

I have also experienced joy in the spiritual realm. I have learned that a soul can be filled with joy even when pleasure, fun, and happiness are absent. The Spirit at times has been so close to me that I have wept with joy during these sacred interactions.

Joy, whether temporal or spiritual, and the fullness of joy are gifts of the Spirit that are given by a loving God in response to our loving Him and keeping His commandments. The unity of spirit and body are required for a fullness of joy. I can't even begin to imagine what a "fullness of joy" will feel like. I have been so overwhelmed by my simple experiences with joy. During the Savior's visit to the new world, he instructed the people to bring their little children to Him and then He knelt in prayer. This is part of the record of that experience:

> *And no tongue can speak, neither can there be written by any man, neither can the hearts of men conceive so great and marvelous things as we both saw and heard Jesus speak; and no one can conceive of the joy which filled our souls at the time we heard him pray for us unto the father.*
>
> *And it came to pass that when Jesus had made an end of praying unto the Father, he arose; but so great was the joy of the multitude that they were overcome.*
>
> *And it came to pass that Jesus spake unto them, and bade them arise.*
>
> *And they arose from the earth, and he said unto them: Blessed are ye because of your faith. And now behold, my joy is full* (3 Nephi 17: 17-20).

I cannot conceive of the joy the multitude felt. Truly beyond my comprehension is the Savior's response that His joy was full. There is much yet for us to experience that will change our lives, our very souls, if we are faithful.

Going Forward

Yea, and cry unto God for all thy support; yea, let all thy doings be unto the Lord, and whithersoever thou goest let it be in the Lord; yea, let all thy thoughts be directed unto the Lord; yea, let the affections of thy heart be placed upon the Lord forever.

Counsel with the Lord in all thy doings, and he will direct thee for good; yea, when thou liest down at night lie down unto the Lord, that he may watch over you in your sleep; and when thou risest in the morning let thy heart be full of thanks unto God; and if ye do these things, ye shall be lifted up at the last day
(Alma 37:36-37, emphasis added).

I have come to know that this direction Alma gave his son, Helaman, is exactly what I need. In fact, I memorized it so that I can keep the counsel near to my thoughts, continually. I recognize that there is much I do not know or comprehend about my life, the mission that may still be in front of me, and God's dealings with His children.

I may not know why some things are required of me, things that may be painful or that are outside of my comfort zone and current opinions. Life has taught me that discomfort is not a sign that what is taking place isn't right or isn't what I should be facing. Am I more worthy than the Savior's apostles, Joseph Smith or any other child of God? Absolutely not. Do I need training, testing, strengthening, chastising and all kinds of experiences, both easy and hard? without a doubt! Now I know why.

Joseph Smith, in the spirit of prophesy, said that God will complete His work and "no unhallowed hand can stop the work from progressing." *(History of the Church, 4:540).* God has stated that

> *. . . this is my work and my glory—to*
> *bring to pass the immortality and eternal*
> *life of man* (Moses 1:39).

I have quoted this scripture several times. What God's work entails is so important in understanding who we are and what is taking place here, right now. My "work" is to become loyal to God and align my life with His will to assist in His work.

I have the feeling that in God's design of mortality, nothing is wasted, no thought, no decision or action, no matter how small it is, everything serves a purpose—a baby's first step, a child writing her own name for the first time, learning to do math, discovering that God hears our prayers, everything is integral to the Plan. The only thing that I see that has no redemptive value is rebellion, unless it is turned to repentance.

This "Godly Economy" begins from the moment of our birth. Think how progressive life is as babies grow to be toddlers and all they have experienced and learned. Then from toddlers to youths and then adults. Every experience, every thought, every insight, every action goes into the makeup of every daughter and son of God. We are who we are, because of them.

Every small, seemingly inconsequential thought, decision, and act is part of our makeup and integral to Father's plan of experience. All of them have the potential to be ennobling, because each one contributes to the whole of the mortal experience, choices determining direction and progression. Even rebels, those who choose to turn from the light to darkness have had the Godly designed mortal experience providing insights and progression that is not possible in the pre-mortal world.

Our discussion has been about recognizing, anxiously seeking, and being willing to own the experiences that move us forward on the path to Eternal Life, God's Life. I believe that it is important to understand that every mortal experience has value if we use it to bring us nearer to Christ and His love. I am thankful for reminders that the small things of life are also a part of God's plan and ought to be appreciated as much as the more striking ones. Once again, I am so moved by this instruction:

Thou shalt thank the Lord thy God in all things (D&C 59:7).

My desire and hope are that before life's end what I ought to do and what I want to do become the same. I now know that everything that God asks me to understand, to do, and to endure is ennobling. He knows my needs far better than I do. I have spent all of my life (without knowing it) trying to catch up with an understanding of God's plan for what is essential in my life and for doing it.

Now that I have had a chance to share my thoughts and testimony regarding life experiences, choices, and Heavenly nurturing, what are your thoughts? What is more important to you, experience or being comfortable? That answer may very well determine what takes place within your life, here on your journey to the Tree of Life.

My prayer for us is that we will "abide in the Savior's love that our joy will be full."

Epilogue – The Garden Allegory

I looked out on the "vegetable garden" area of our yard, where for decades we have raised plants that have been a delight to the eye and have given us food that has been life-sustaining. This year, the garden is covered with an assortment of weeds of many types that threaten to entirely take over in defiance of the original purpose for this garden area. It is obvious that this plot of earth, set aside to help with our nutritional needs, has been left to the whims and notions of Mother Nature. Wind, animals, and other passing sources have left seeds for germination that do not comply with the vision of healthy food that we have had for this ground.

The reason? The caretakers, the gardeners, those with invested desires to make the property productive in its potential have obviously failed to give the care needed to maintain its productivity. She, who loved making a patch of earth beautiful and productive had to retire from her efforts, having sustained a stroke that robbed her of physical ability. My wife is no longer able to able to plant, tend, or harvest what this ground is capable of producing. Unfortunately, she has an assistant, that would be me, whose back rebels when he has been on his knees for more than short periods of time. Sadly, the potential is unrealized as care has defaulted to elements and factors lacking the same positive purposes.

It is sad to see vegetation taking up the space and nutrients that could be going to plants that would be a blessing to us, either as beauty or food or both. This is all happening, because focused and determined care has been abandoned, leaving the ground open to any adversarial use that comes by. Those seeds/plants that don't need care to sprout and thrive are usually the ones that grow without invitation, needing additional care and provide no value for anyone. It is interesting that generally in life the "plants" that would nourish our souls require much in the way of cultivating effort and care in order to be productive. Those that have little or no worth are the ones that take over on their own, producing nothing of redeeming value.

Isn't this situation symbolic of what happens when we do not provide care, cultivating those influences and elements in our lives that produce essential, productive growth, progression on the paths of life that truly bless our lives and the lives of others. The productive life path also is focused on producing worthiness to complete the God-given missions we were each given before coming to earth. Fulfilling those requirements and completing our faithful path of life mission qualifies us to be worthy to return Home to Father and Christ.

What happens to each of us individually when we pay little attention to choosing what life experiences pass across the portals to our minds and hearts, without tending or making choices for our wellbeing and productivity? When we do little or nothing about investing in and using our potential and our "fertile soil," no matter what possibilities exist, aren't we in the same place that my garden is in? Haven't we turned our decision-making over to some other power whose influence will likely not be in our best interest?

What do we expect as the outcome when any thought, any idea, no matter whether it is positive or negative crosses the threshold of our minds and hearts and we do nothing about it? Haven't we effectively given permission for it to land in our personal "fertile soil," take root, and influence our lives without care or consideration? We can only expect the results to be chaotic productions of emotions, interests, habits, and efforts, whether good or bad, but how can we tell the difference anyway? Our souls (comprised of body and spirit) need nourishment continually from our personal efforts and "plantings" in order to thrive. Call the required nourishment spiritual and mortal, or divine and human, or infinite and finite, we are composed of more than earth elements and need the sustaining gifts of nutrients for body and spirit.

We are the spirit children of our Heavenly Father clothed within a mortal frame provided by our earthly parents. Perhaps it would be valuable to us if we could see ourselves as we are seen by Father and Christ. They are the Gardeners. We are the plants. Do we readily and anxiously receive all the nourishment They provide by "watering and feeding" all of us, the "garden plants" with that which will satiate, strengthen, and prepare us for the Harvest to come; when the growth of each "plant" will be examined and all of those who have grown into vital and worthwhile fruit will be harvested and invited to Their table.

BIBLIOGRAPHY

The Holy Bible, Salt Lake City, Utah, USA, The Church of Jesus Christ of Latter-day Saints, 2013, © By Intellectual Reserve, Inc.

The Book of Mormon, Salt Lake City, Utah, USA, The Church of Jesus Christ of Latter-day Saints, 2013, © By Intellectual Reserve, Inc.

The Doctrine And Covenants Of The Church of Jesus Christ of Latter-day Saints, Salt Lake City, Utah, USA, The Church of Jesus Christ of Latter-day Saints, 2013, © By Intellectual Reserve, Inc.

The Pearl Of Great Price, Salt Lake City, Utah, USA, The Church of Jesus Christ of Latter-day Saints, 2013, © By Intellectual Reserve, Inc.

Books by *Michael Steven Purles*

One-Day Miracles - Change Your Brain to Master Your Weight

Turtletoes - Following the Steps of An Angel

Called to Discipleship:

> Becometh as a Child

> Turning to Christ With Full Purpose of Heart

> Embrace Ennobling Experiences

To know more about the author and his works,

please visit **michaelpurles.com**

ABOUT THE AUTHOR

Michael Steven Purles is an author who has served as a business skills trainer, as well as a business manager throughout much of his adult life. His writing opportunities have followed two parallel but different pathways, one for business and the other for personal life experiences. You will recognize in his writing a specific focus on finding strength for and helping to lift burdens that are a part of each person's life. A special focus is on our personal relationship with Jesus Christ and becoming one of His true disciples.

www.ingramcontent.com/pod-product-compliance
Lightning Source LLC
Chambersburg PA
CBHW060342130626
46553CB00003B/1087